WHAT ABOUT CHRISTIAN ROCK?

WHAT ABOUT CHRISTIAN ROCK?

Dan Peters, Steve Peters
and **Cher Merrill**

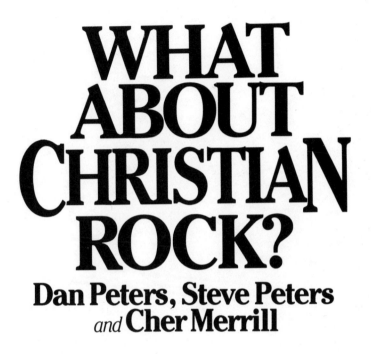

BETHANY HOUSE PUBLISHERS
MINNEAPOLIS, MINNESOTA 55438
A Division of Bethany Fellowship, Inc.

Published by Bethany House Publishers
A Division of Bethany Fellowship, Inc.
6820 Auto Club Road, Minneapolis, Minnesota 55438

Printed in the United States of America

Library of Congress Cataloging-in-Publication Data

Peters, Dan.
   What about Christian rock?

   Bibliography: p.
   1. Christian rock music—History and criticism.
I. Peters, Steve.   II. Merrill, Cher.   III. Title.
ML3187.5.P47   1986   783.6   86-24472
ISBN 0-87123-672-9 (pbk.)

Dedication

This book is dedicated to a legion of prayer warriors including:
Bill, Shelley, Becky, Julie, Renae, Angela, Melody,
Nathan, Ruth Ann, Matthew, Donalda, Mary Lou, Barb,
Sue, Bernie, Jack, Judy W., Carole, Judy F., Ruth,
Mom and Dad Peters, People of Praise,
and Zion Christian Center.
Thank you.

Dan and Steve Peters
Cher Merrill

"Make a joyful noise unto the Lord, all the earth;
make a loud noise and rejoice, and sing praise" (Ps. 98:4).

Contents

Preface

I was sitting at a church concert. There were guitars and drums, and they were playing rock music! It caught me off guard. And then the girl—a successful rock performer—shared about her deliverance from drugs. Next a man got up and said, "No matter what you've done, you can be pure again, as if you've never sinned, new all over again."

And I thought, *He's talking about a major heart transplant, folks!* And I was shook! I went and hid in the ladies room, because I was gonna cry. I had to get myself back together.

But when I came out, a Christian sister met me and she said, "Would you like to think about accepting Jesus?"

And that did it! I couldn't hold back any longer. It was my night!

And that's the exciting thing at Christian concerts—it's somebody's night. It was my night back in September, 1971. It's somebody's night tonight.

Wendi Kaiser
Rez Band

Introduction

Since the first Truth About Rock Seminar in 1979, we have received the Christian community's enthusiastic approval for alerting young people to secular rock music's excesses. Through countless articles, interviews and personal appearances—ranging from the *700 Club* to *ABC Nightline*, from *Rolling Stone* to *Contemporary Christian Music*—we have attacked pop music's many immoral lyrics, lifestyles, goals and graphics. And Christians nationwide have applauded us for it.

Now, we hope to bring the same carefully documented research and calm rationale to the highly controversial issue of "Christian rock." We release this book, however, with some hesitation, fearing it will be ill-received by many Christians who have already made up their minds.

For too long, people for and against Christian rock have hurled insults and accusations at each other. But the Bible reminds us to "speak evil of no one, to avoid quarreling, to be gentle, and to show perfect courtesy toward all men" (Titus 3:2, RSV). Consequently, we hope you will carefully weigh the evidence presented here, remembering your responsibility to pursue truth rather than prejudice.

While we will offer some observations and guidelines, we don't intend to pronounce a verdict on Christian contemporary music, but simply to provide an open forum for those involved in the music to speak for themselves. Please hear them out as they reveal their motives, explain their methods and answer their accusers. Whether you choose to agree or disagree, find out why some choose to dress so unconventionally and play so raucously. Familiarize yourself with their lyrics, investigate their lifestyles, search their hearts.

As you read, remember God is the ultimate judge; He will hand down the final verdict. Adopt the attitude the teacher Gamaliel demanded of the Jewish council when it first persecuted the early church: "Let them alone; for if this plan or this undertaking is of men, it will fail; but if it is of God, you will not be able to overthrow them. You might even be found opposing God! (Acts 5:38, 39, RSV).

When you have heard all the arguments from both sides, close the book. Think about it. Pray about it. Then decide for yourself, "What about Christian rock?"

Part One

Changing Your Tune

Chapter One

Rock Music: A Killer

*If you want to reach young people in this country,
write a song . . .*

—*Sociologist Serge Denisoff*

Dear Peters Brothers,

I was at your seminar when you began to play examples of what you called "Christian" contemporary music—as an alternative to secular rock music. Well, I grabbed my children and headed for the door, because the small portion I heard looked and sounded just like the ungodly music you had just been knocking! I don't understand! One minute you are condemning rock and roll and the next you are offering young people the same perversion, the same demonic beat and rebellious sound under a different label! You are Christians and say you are concerned for the well-being of our children. Don't you realize that music is a "wolf in sheep's clothing" and could never be pleasing to God?

A Concerned Parent

Is contemporary Christian music (CCM) a ravenous wolf in disguise, or is it pleasing to God? Is the description "Christian rock" a contradiction in terms, or is it a legitimate, edifying art form? Are Christian rock artists just as deluded and deluding as their mainstream counterparts, or do they perform a vital ministry in which the Lord takes great pleasure? In short, what about Christian rock?

In our ministry, we have always tried to provide the information and criteria both parents and young people need to make reasoned, biblical decisions about their music. However, inquiries such as the preceding one—some indignantly protesting, some honestly seeking answers—have given us reason to more deeply analyze and pray about the whole issue of gospel rock.

Now, more than ever, we see an urgent need for parents, teens, pastors and performing artists to reflect the attitude of the Lord when He invited us, "Come now, let us reason together . . . (Isa. 1:18, RSV). It is time for a thorough examination of the real issues. It is time we went beyond the beat, the look or sound of the music to hear and discuss what is actually being said. We need to objectively, yet critically, assess the music on the same bases used to judge secular music: its lyrics, lifestyles, goals and graphics.

We sincerely hope this book will provide a common ground on which to do just that: to lovingly and calmly discuss the subject of Christian rock. We don't claim to have all the answers. In fact, we authors have not always agreed on every issue. But, we do think we can give some helpful insights and guidelines for discussing this sometimes controversial issue, as well as raise some interesting topics for discussion.

Before we examine Christian music, however, we need to briefly look at the message and influence of its counterpart—secular rock. The contrast it provides will help us gain some needed perspective on music in general, an educated viewpoint from which to deal with the question of Christian rock.

Pop Music Porn Wars

Recording artist Frank Zappa says his tune, "Porn Wars"—a 12-minute satire poking fun at a Senate committee hearing—will never carry an industry-approved label warning of explicit lyrical content. The hearing had investigated secular rock music's promotion of drugs, sex and violence, and Zappa contends that "the way to solve problems is not to blame everything on rock 'n' roll."[1]

Admittedly, an occasional witch-hunting preacher or fren-

---

[1] Barry Massey, *Associated Press* (11/1/85).

zied parent has gone too far, blaming rock music for every teen-age ill from acne to rebellion. In truth, rock music is the language of a culture born and bred in the age of electronic communication. What T. S. Eliot once said of literature now applies to pop music: "There was never a time when the reading [now listening] public was so large, or so helplessly exposed to the influences of its own time."

Likewise, Pope Paul VI saw the mass media, and music in particular, as a cause of the world's leading problems, describing it as "the deafening roar of a thousand voices which fill the atmosphere of modern life." Even Frank Zappa admits pop music wields a powerful influence. He once boasted, "I'm the devil's advocate. We have our own worshippers who are called 'groupies.' Girls will give their bodies to musicians as you would give a sacrifice to a god."[2]

Zappa's flamboyant remarks can hardly pass as expert opinion. Others more qualified to judge, however, have made headlines when they linked rock music's influence not only to general trends but to specific violent deaths and assaults, as well as the suicides of some of its most avid fans:

- *New York Post:* Homicide chief, as well as local teens, blame rock videos for brutal cult killing.
- *Toronto Sun:* Authorities announce Iron Maiden fan shot and killed policeman and wounded two others before dying in shootout.
- *United Press International:* Suit filed against rock star Ozzy Osbourne claims 19-year-old John McCollum committed suicide at urging of Osbourne song, "Suicide Solution."
- *U.S. News & World Report:* Richard Ramirez, charged with 16 "Night Stalker" murders on West Coast, said by friends to have been obsessed by satanic themes in music of heavy-metal band AC/DC and its album "Highway to Hell."
- *United Press International:* Chief deputy medical examiner says Pink Floyd's morbid lyrics and melodies may have contributed to ritualistic suicide of 18-year-old St. John's Military Academy cadet.

Isolated incidents? Perhaps, but since Satan is described in

---

[2]As quoted by LaMar Boschman, in *The Rebirth of Music*, (Little Rock, Ark.: Manasseh Books, 1980), p. 20.

Scripture as a thief who "comes only in order to steal, kill, and destroy" (John 10:10, GNB), it is not surprising that he would twist the powerful medium of music into a tool of his deathly trade.

Some people, sighting somewhat sketchy evidence from plant and animal studies, say Satan's tool is the beat of rock music; others indict noisome rock's ear-assaulting volume. Still others throw stones at rock for any and every reason. One pastor says its real harm stems from its "wild, loud, carefree, hysterical, hard-rock style of music."

While we plan to discuss some of these ideas later in the book, secular rock music's problems go much deeper than any of these theories would indicate. Music—any music—has the power to affect us through four much more basic ways, and those four aspects can be used to determine if it is fatally flawed or twisted, if it is capable of being used as a tool of Satan. Those four areas, discussed in detail in *Why Knock Rock?*, are its lyrics, lifestyles, goals and graphics.

The Four Fatal Flaws Revisited

Lyrics

Most young people contend they really don't hear lyrics. Studies have shown, however, that 62 percent of all high school students listen to rock music regularly, averaging 6 to 7 hours per day (and of course, comprehension increases with repeated listening). Consequently, although most fans are initially attracted to a tune's sound or popularity, 27 percent of rock's regular listeners look for and understand the meaning behind the lyrics.[3] Furthermore, teens often pick up lyrics and meanings to popular songs through radio disc jockeys and fan magazines.

Despite the overwhelming evidence that these modern-day educators hold unprecedented sway over youth, those in the know admit most of today's rock heroes sing and write with their eyes on cash dividends, not culture destruction. Says Sid Bern-

[3]Michael Quirke, *Rock Music and Drug Abuse in Young People*, Bureau of Alcohol and Other Drug Abuse, State of Wisconsin (2/82), p. 11.

stein, the New York music veteran who arranged the Beatles' first U.S. tour: "The importance of sensationalism and a lack of originality have given birth to violence and sex, because that's where the dollars are."[4]

Lifestyles

Undoubtedly, few mainstream rock stars live out the bizarre images and antics they promote on stage or through fan magazines. In fact, one heavy metal group, Quiet Riot, blatantly admits they will do anything to get a crowd going. So much for sincerity.

However, when a *World Almanac and Book of Facts* survey asked 4,000 high schoolers to name their heroes, included in the top eight were Prince, Madonna, Bruce Springsteen, Eddie Van Halen and Debbie Allen of the rock-filled show, *Fame.* Young people seriously view these and other rock stars as their modern-day heroes, and yet most mainstream rock artists demonstrate blatant irresponsibility with their rock 'n' roll images.

Speaking of the shoddy role-modeling of some of today's rock superstars such as Madonna, Christian artist Amy Grant said, "If we get to the end and the whole thing was a joke and she was just putting it on to make a few bucks, then I'll say, 'Madonna, why'd you do that? You confused everybody. Little girls really wanted to be just like you and that really wasn't you after all. You were just playing a game.' If it was a game, then that was her choice. For me it's not a game."[5]

It's not a game for our young people, either. According to *U.S. News & World Report,* studies show that teenagers listen to an estimated 10,500 hours of rock music between the seventh and the eleventh grades alone—just 500 hours fewer than the total hours they spend in school over 12 years.[6] They are searching for role models, and they deserve something better than most of what secular rock music has to offer. They need some real heroes.

Goals

As noted, some rock groups simply take the money and run.

[4]*U.S. News & World Report* (10/28/85), p. 48.
[5]"The Gavin Interview: Amy Grant," *The Gavin Report,* (6/7/85), p. 23.
[6]*U.S. News & World Report* (10/28/85), p. 46.

Dee Snider of Twisted Sister admits, "Our philosophy has always been to do anything to become famous."[7] Other groups, such as Britannia's Bronski Beat, have political and social statements to make. On their aptly named first album, *The Age of Consent,* which rose to the top of the British charts, they not only expound on their open sexuality, but promote a nihilistic view of life as well. Says former Beat member, Jimmy Somerville, "That made me really proud . . . because of the kind of record it was. I never expected to see an album of gay love songs reach the top position."[8]

Still other groups seem to have little or no idea why they exist or what—if indeed anything—they stand for. As Mötley Crüe's bassist, Nikki Sixx, crassly puts it, "We're the American youth. And youth is about sex, drugs, pizzas, and more sex. We're intellectuals on a crotch level."[9]

Graphics

Noting the value of album cover art (or perhaps the lack of value of his music), England's punk rocker Johnny Rotten, formerly of the Sex Pistols, says, "If people bought the records for the music, this thing would have died a death long ago."[10] Whether they are purchased for the music or the art, however, a visit to your local record shop will convince you LP covers betray a fondness for the darker themes of life.

Displaying racy album covers of such artists as Wendy O. Williams, Mötley Crüe and WASP, Tipper Gore of the Parent Music Resource Center (PMRC) said to a Senate committee that though there are many causes for teen suicide, pregnancy and rape, "it is our contention that pervasive messages aimed at children which promote and glorify suicide, rape and sadomasochism have to be numbered among the contributing factors."

The PMRC members have also set their sights on seamy video clips, putting pressure on the industry to have a warning noted before any objectionable video is played on Music TeleVision

---

[7]*Spin* (5/85), p. 10.
[8]*Spin* (2/86), p. 18.
[9]*Single Times* (7–8/85), p. 14.
[10]*The 2nd Album Cover Album* (New York: A & W Visual Library, 1982), p. 23.

(MTV) or similar video programs.

Certainly, the importance of graphics in rock videos can't be understated, and even the industry is willing to admit it needs to begin to regulate itself. In his address before the Second Annual Video/Musical Seminar, Danny Goldberg, president of Gold Mountain Records, warned, "We're on the cutting edge of culture and responsible for the world of the future."[11]

Likewise, veteran rock performer Bob Dylan admits, "It used to be that people would buy a record if they liked what they heard on the radio, but video has changed a lot of that. If someone comes along now with a new song, people talk about, 'Well, what does it look like?' "[12]

Despite its importance, however, rock music's graphics continue to decline in both content and quality. The National Coalition on Television Violence (NCTV) reports over half of the videos shown on MTV feature or strongly imply violence—usually of a sexual nature. The NCTV's studies indicate incidents of violence occur on MTV at the rate of 18 per hour.

Once again, as far as the record industry is concerned, considerations such as morals or even good taste are beside the point; money is the motivator. Says video producer Ken Walz, "When you ask are we supposed to be moral, are we supposed to be humanistic, are we supposed to titillate . . . we're *supposed* to be none of those things. What we are supposed to do is . . . sell records, concert tickets and artists."[13]

Reaching Today's Youth

According to Serge Denisoff, a sociologist and popular music expert from Bowling Green University, "If you want to reach young people in this country, write a song, don't buy an ad."[14] The question is, once Satan reaches our youth through secular rock music's four flaws, what is he teaching them? To answer

[11]*Rock Video* (Vol. 8, 12/84), p. 8.
[12]Robert Hilburn, *Los Angeles Times*, as noted in *St. Paul Pioneer Press and Dispatch* (11/17/85), p. 9E.
[13]Serge Denisoff, as quoted by Michael Quirke, op. cit., p. 3.
[14]*Newsweek* (12/30/85), p. 54.

that question (and to provide a stark contrast to the Christian rock alternatives examined later), let's check out current rock heroes—from mellow to metal—and discover the musical lessons they teach.

Chapter Two

The Rock-Hard Facts

Most young people are looking for lives to copy. . . . You have to see somebody that you admire and that you want to copy.

—Psychologist Kenneth E. Clark

As we travel the country giving our Why Knock Rock? seminar, a majority of both parents and teens express surprise at the sort of material we present in this chapter, documentation and lyrics produced by today's rock "heroes." Most people, it seems, are paying little attention, allowing rock's influence to infiltrate their homes unrestrained.

Experts are painfully aware, however, of both music and its persuasive powers. Dr. Joseph Novello, director of a drug program in Washington, says he frequently asks his teenage patients, "To what kind of music do you listen?" Whether it is drug- or sexually-oriented, satanic or sadistic, Novello believes the patient's favorite music denotes his frame of mind.

How bad can music be? The examples on the following pages will show you. They are similar to what we present in our seminar and in our book, *Why Knock Rock?* If you're not familiar with this information, we strongly advise you read it, but be warned: It will shock you!

Rock Roll Call

Accept: "Let's plug a bomb in everyone's arse," Udo Dirkschneider sings in the title song of their LP, *Balls to the Wall.* Their tune "Head over Heels" deals with voyeurism, while "London Leatherboys" and "Love Child" tell of homosexual eroticism.

23

Bon Jovi: Describing a drinking jag while on tour with Mötley Crüe, Jon Bon Jovi brags, "We had probably gone through two or three bottles [of Jack Daniels] by then, and . . . we were smashing everything in that bar. . . . We started to walk out when hotel security stopped us and handed us a bill for $5,000. We just handed it to our manager and headed to a whore house up the block."[1]

Bowie: In "Modern Love," David Bowie sings, "Church on time terrifies me . . . church on time makes me put my trust in God and man."

Boy George: The summer of 1986 was not a good one for pop singer Boy George, lead singer of Culture Club. In July, he pleaded guilty to heroin possession, was fined $375, and began the drug rehabilitation treatment previously used by rock stars Pete Townshend and Eric Clapton. In August, songwriter/keyboard player Michael Rudetsky, a friend of George's, was found dead in the flamboyant British singer's London mansion.

DeBarge: Songwriter Bunny DeBarge insists, "I pray to God before I write them [songs], and ask God to give me the words." Yet they plead in one tune, "You've got to please me/My body's burnin' for your love/. . . gotta get a little/I know you're gonna love it."[2]

Dire Straits: Their *Brothers in Arms* LP—which debuted as number one on the British charts—included a tune which says, "See the little faggot with the earring and the makeup . . . that little faggot, he's a millionaire."

Duran Duran: Duran Duran's Simon le Bon says of sex: "It's always been an important part of Duran's songs. It's always been the most important thing on my mind." Pointing out the lyrics of their James Bond theme song, "Dance into the Fire," he says: They're like sex-assassination lyrics . . . 'dance' being the sexual metaphor and the 'fire' being danger, obviously."[3]

[1] *Hit Parader* (5/85), p. 61.
[2] *Record* (2/84), p. 62.
[3] *Star Hits* (9/85), p. 7.

Easton: Sheena Easton's hit, "Sugar Walls," a tune written by Prince for her *A Private Heaven* LP, dispenses with metaphor and gets right to the point: "Come spend the night inside my sugar walls. Take advantage, it's all right/ . . . Your body's on fire, admit it."

E-Street Band: "I used to do a lot of drugs," says Clarence Clemmons, the most famous member of Bruce Springsteen's E-Street Band. "All kinds," he adds, "heavy stuff, too." The sweet-playing saxophonist credits his cold-turkey cure to the teachings of Sri Chimoy, an Indian guru.[4]

Frankie Goes To Hollywood: This international band's hit single, "Two Tribes," begins with the eerie words, "Mine is the last voice that you will ever hear," and then adds, "Sex and horror are the new gods." On the slip inside the album, *Welcome to the Pleasuredome*, they write, "Manipulation of children's minds in the field of religion or politics would touch off a parental storm and a rash of Congressional investigations. But in the world of commerce, children are fair game and legitimate prey."

Golden Earring: In their "Twilight Zone" video, the group features a macabre background scene of torture and murder sequences.

Houston: Definitely the darling of the 1985 American Music Awards, Whitney Houston praises marital infidelity in the hit, "Saving All My Love for You": "A few stolen moments is all that we share/You've got your family/And they need you there . . . My friends try and tell me find a man of your own, but . . . I'm saving all my love for you."

Idol: In "Rebel Yell" Billy Idol sings, "Last night a little angel came pumping on the floor/She said, 'Oh baby, I got a license for love' "; in his "White Wedding" video Idol viciously forces a ring on his "bride's" finger as blood gushes over her hand.

Keel: Formed in 1984, this hard-rocking band now has two LP's, the second produced by KISS's Gene Simmons. In the title song,

---

[4]*Minneapolis Star and Tribune* (12/20/85), p. 19C.

"The Right to Rock," they defiantly shout, "Don't let anyone tell you/How to live your life. We won't turn it off, we won't turn it down/'Cause it's our way of life."

Lauper: Rock's fun girl Cyndi Lauper admitted to *Rolling Stone* magazine that the inspiration for her video/single, "She Bop," was a homosexual sex-fantasy magazine, *Blueboy,* and that the tune promotes masturbation.[5]

Madonna: "As long as I'm riding high on the charts, I don't care if they call me trashy, a tart or a slut," says the sensual rock queen whose concert performances *People* magazine headlined, "The Show Is Sex." Though she quietly accepted the printing of her nude photos in *Penthouse* and *Playboy,* she drew the line when a five-year-old porno flick in which she performed was resurrected.[6]

Manowar: Ozzy Osbourne beware: There's more than one way to make a lasting impression on record producers! This heavy metal quartet signed their recording contract in quill pens dipped in their own blood.[7]

Mellencamp: In "Serious Business," John Cougar Mellencamp exposes the shallow, meaningless world of rock and roll, but offers no alternatives: "Take my life/Take my soul/ . . . This is serious business/Sex and violence and rock 'n' roll." In another song he sings, "I been doin' it since I was a young kid and I come out grinnin'/I fight authority, authority always wins."

Mötley Crüe: Vince Neil (Wharton), the group's lead singer, was ordered to pay $2.6 million to the victims of an accident that killed a passenger in his car, Nicholas Dingley (a member of a band called Hanoi Rocks), and seriously injured two occupants of another car. Neil, who was speeding and under the influence of alcohol, was also sentenced to 200 hours of community service, five years' probation, and thirty days in jail.[8]

---

[5]*Rolling Stone* (7/19/84), p. 8.
[6]*Globe* (6/6/85), p. 37.
[7]*Rock Collector's Edition*, Vol. 2.
[8]*Minneapolis Star and Tribune* (1/9/85) and *Rolling Stone* (11/7/85), p. 20.

Moyet: Described by *Rolling Stone* as its 1985 choice for Female Vocalist, Alison "Alf" Moyet's first solo album includes a double-entendre tune, "Love Resurrection." She told *Melody Maker* magazine, "I don't say, 'Take me, take me, take me.' I say, 'Ooooh! Drop your drawers, you b——!' "[9]

Newton-John: Once the sweetheart of the country-pop set, Olivia Newton-John changed all that with her scorching LP's, *Physical* and *Soul Kiss.* She makes it clear sex is her selling tool in the tune, "Overnight Observation," in which a doctor seduces a woman patient, and in the title tune of *Soul Kiss,* when she sighs passionately as she sings of oral sex.

Osbourne: To those who contend Ozzy Osbourne's negative music can lead to suicidal thoughts in impressionable teens, the werewolf-in-sheep's-skin says "ba-a-ah": "Parents have called me and said, 'When my son died of a drug overdose, your record was on the turntable.' I can't help that. These people are freaking out anyway, and they need a vehicle for freak-outs."[10]

Parker: Charged by Huey Lewis with blatantly stealing "I Want a New Drug" for his hit, "Ghostbusters" (the issue was settled out of court), Ray Parker Jr.'s next album, *Sex and the Single Man*, is described by music critic Rick Shefchik as the "slimiest soul-rock on the shelves today." In "I'm a Dog," Parker complains, "You should have left me alone/Because you knew I was a dog before you took my bone."

The Pointer Sisters: Scoring hit after hit, the Pointers sing in "I'm So Excited," "I want to squeeze you, please you/I just can't get enough/And if you move real slow/I'll let it go."

Power Station: Featuring two of Duran Duran's glamour boys, this hybrid group sings, "You're dirty and sweet, clad in black, don't look back . . . You're slim and weak/ . . . Get it on, bang a gong."

Prince: Though many fans claim that Prince is a changed man,

---

[9]*Rolling Stone* (2/28/85), p. 41.
[10]*Life* (12/84), p. 112.

much less explicit in his lyric content, his records and concerts still sizzle with sex. Selling an astounding 2.5 million copies before promotion, Prince's *Around the World* LP features the hit single, "Raspberry Beret": "They say the first time ain't the greatest/But I'll tell u if I had the chance 2 do it all again/I wouldn't change a stroke/'Cause baby I'm the most."

Scorpion: From their popular *Love at First Sting* LP comes the tempestuous "Rock You Like a Hurricane": "So what is wrong with another sin/The bitch is hungry, she needs to tell/So I give her inches and feed her well."

Shalamar: Howard Hewett, Jr., former lead singer of the pop/ soul group, was charged with possessing and distributing cocaine. If convicted, he faces a maximum penalty of a $405,000 fine and 49 years in prison. Hewett had a $300,000 recording contract awaiting his signature when he was arrested.[11]

The Smiths: Says lead singer Patrick Morrissey of the almost "Messianic" power of rock music, "Many people underestimate it as a force; this is dramatically wrong. It is the last refuge for the young people; no other platform has so much exposure."[12]

Springsteen: While he claims to stand for traditional values, mournfully depressing tunes can be found even on Bruce Springsteen's most upbeat, *Born in the U.S.A.* Says Christian artist Loyd Boldman of Springsteen's brooding, "Springsteen has so much assessment of where people are, but not where they should go." Though described as a working class hero, Springsteen is not above taking a cheap shot as he croons "I'm on Fire": "Hey little girl is your daddy home/Did he go and leave you all alone?/ I got a bad desire/Oh, I'm on fire."

Tears for Fears: "Adolescence," says *Rolling Stone* of the Tears for Fears' bass player, "was not Curt Smith's idea of a good time. His parents separated when he was very young." To get attention, the article says, he took up a life of petty crime and vandalism.[13]

---

[11]*Minneapolis Star and Tribune* (1/17/86), p. 14A.
[12]*People* (6/24/85), p. 105.
[13]*Rolling Stone* (7/1/85), p. 71.

'Til Tuesday: In their "Voices Carry" video, a sneering boyfriend first accuses lead singer Aimee Mann, then tries to rape her. Though self-defense would have been appropriate, the girl finally gives in.[14]

Turner: The 44-year-old godmother of raunch and roll, Tina Turner, is still telling teens about "love": "Though the touch of your hand/Makes my pulse react/ . . . it's only the thrill of boy meeting girl/ . . . It's physical/ . . . What's love got to do with it?" Meanwhile, her ex-husband and musician, Ike Turner, was jailed in West Hollywood, California, for cocaine possession after being pulled over for a traffic violation. A search of his car revealed a loaded pistol, drug paraphernalia and a "sizable amount of cocaine."[15]

Wham!: The British duo Wham! visited China in 1985. However, the flight to Canton for their second scheduled concert was turned back when the bands trumpeter Raoul de Oliveira suddenly plunged a knife into his own stomach. Though Oliveira was described by co-manager Jazz Summers as having hallucinated, it was later claimed no drugs were involved.[16]

Winning Souls While Pleasing Saints

What should a parent do about such music? Dr. Novello says parents are obligated to know about their children's musical preferences and "if you take exception to the words, don't allow them to listen."[17] Unfortunately that approach provides no musical alternatives. This results in a vacuum in which no one can survive, and teenagers are no exception.

Others would categorically condemn any music simply due to its beat or sound, believing as one prominent evangelist puts it, "Any Christian who would allow any type of rock or country recording in his home is inviting in the powers of darkness. By compromising with this satanic influence, overt control of the

---

[14]*Rock Video Idols* (8/85), p. 27.
[15]*Minneapolis Star and Tribune* (1/13/86), p. 9A and *Sun-Sentinel* (1/13/86), p. 2A.
[16]*Newsweek* (4/22/85), p. 44.
[17]Kandy Stroud, "Stop Pornographic Rock," *Newsweek* (5/6/85), p. 14.

mind and spirit is possible. *Anyone listening to this filth is openly entering into communion with evil spirits.* All of the rock music (and probably all, or at least most, of the country music) being aired today is demonically inspired."

While we certainly don't want anyone to play around with evil spirits, this sort of attitude borders on musical paranoia and leaves no room for reasonable discussion. Consequently, a great deal of misunderstanding and bitterness can develop.

What Paul Baker says in his history of Christian contemporary music, describing the self-righteous objections of many adults to the so-called "Jesus music" of the early sixties, still holds true today: "What those often well-meaning adults didn't realize was that by so dogmatically renouncing rock with no ifs, ands, or buts, they were giving young people a blatant black or white alternative: rock or religion."[18]

Ken Gaub, who has given his life to providing wholesome, Christian entertainment for young people, pinpointed the problem when he said, "The toughest thing to do is to win souls and please saints at the same time."[19]

So, instead of being unnecessarily dogmatic, let's approach the subject of rock music seeking God's wisdom. For as James tells us, God's wisdom is peaceful, gentle, friendly, full of compassion and free from prejudice, producing a harvest of good deeds. "And goodness," he adds, "is the harvest that is produced from the seeds the peacemakers plant in peace" (James 3:17, 18, GNB).

The peace James refers to doesn't come when a teenager's stereo is turned off for good, but when we talk about the issues and together carefully seek God's answers. So let's discuss the issues fairly and calmly. Let's all work to discover God's will in the area of music. And if we find there are issues on which we don't see eye-to-eye, let's agree to disagree agreeably. It's an important topic, one that should concern us all, parent and child. After all, as Martin Luther once said, "The devil has no right to all the good tunes"; or as Christian entertainer Larry Norman paraphrased it, "Why should the devil have all the good music?"

---

[18]Paul Baker, *Contemporary Christian Music*, (Westchester, Ill.: Crossway Books, 1979), p. 43.
[19]Steve Haggerty, "On the Road For God," *Charisma* (11/85), p. 81.

Chapter Three

We Need Some Heroes

Whether Christians like it or not, rock is definitely going to mark the last half of the twentieth century with things that are going to be there for the next four or five centuries.

—*Calvin Miller*

From the anti-Vietnam War rock rallies of the sixties to the rockers-for-food festivals of the mid-eighties, modern rock heroes have used their positions of power to peddle their ideas to the world—sometimes for the better, more often, for the worse. Undeniably, ending the tragedy of war and feeding starving babies are good causes. However, one has to wonder about the rock superstars involved. Why do they exhibit such great concern for children in other lands, and yet demonstrate little interest in the moral/spiritual welfare of youngsters in their own country?

Could money be the key? Christian performer Steve Taylor says, "You know back in the late sixties and early seventies, at least you had somebody that hopefully had some kind of moral basis for what they were singing about. I feel today, with some of the projects we have seen like 'We Are the World,' you get performers that will sing for charitable causes . . . because it will help further their career. You have people in music in general that are totally interested in money and nothing else."

These talented performers create music that sways generations of opinions. They have opportunities to encourage and support their fans, to challenge young people to strive for excellence. They have the potential to be trusted "companions," helping teens through the difficulties of growing up. And yet, these modern-day pied pipers choose to sing of disenchantment, distrust, drugs and dirty deeds.

Ratt lead singer Stephen Pearcy boasts, "Ratt is about party-ing, sex and heroes."[1] Likewise, Rick James announced about his starring film role, "It'll be about my life. Sex and drugs and rock 'n' roll. And *reality*."[2]

Are these our heroes, our champions? Their lyrics, at best, offer shallow answers to some of life's deepest problems. At worst, they teach lies and foolishness. Heroes such as Pearcy and James demonstrate the kind of courage that comes from a bottle or syringe, and promote promiscuity and reckless rebellion as desirable behavior.

Perhaps the greatest sin, though, is that they masquerade behind a glamorous, seductive image when many of their lives are filled with loneliness, drugs, emptiness—even premature death. In a more honest moment, Journey's drummer Steve Smith admitted, "All rock stars are afraid of not seeming bigger than life and that's why they get screwed up."[3] Accept's Stefan Kaufmann isn't willing to take the blame, but does admit *others* have problems: "There are some bands who are potentially dan-gerous, and I think they don't know what they're doing, which is bad, or don't care, which is worse."[4]

Steve Taylor takes the thought a bit further with his tune, "You've Been Bought." Says Taylor about the song, "A lot of performers are taking on this posture of Satanism—or some-thing like that—when they have no belief in the devil, no belief in hell . . . or they do videos with a lot of sexism or violence. They say it's a joke, but we know the kids take it seriously. The point I tried to make with that song is to warn young people that a lot of these guys are doing things out of money motivation, they're acting like they're something that they're not. . . . They really have no belief in that at all. It's very dangerous because money is the motivation."

---

[1]*Life* (12/84), p. 106.
[2]*Record* (10/85), p. 10.
[3]*Circus* (10/31/82).
[4]*Rock Video Idols* (8/85), p. 76.

The Antihero

Undoubtedly, most of today's rock artists would be better described antiheroes. They seem to represent just the opposite of what we look for in traditional heroes, striking out against society or looking out for "number one." And yet, despite their self-serving outlook—or perhaps because of it—these reverse heroes are able to "steal, kill and destroy" young lives.

Does that sound a bit farfetched? Not to veteran rocker David Crosby. He once actually boasted he could steal kids from their parents. "By saying that, I'm not talking about kidnapping," he explained. "I'm just talking about changing their value systems, which removes them from their parents' world very effectively."[5] Though Crosby no longer seems to pose a great threat—his cocaine addiction has cost him his health, friends and fortune—his cavalier attitude typifies that of many rock artists.

Psychiatrist Dr. Robert E. Litman says this type of negligent notion is deplorable: "My greatest criticism of popular music aimed at young persons is that of irresponsibility and lack of leadership." Litman doesn't fault all rock musicians but admits, "The main danger is that many young people may echo the attitudes of such singers whom they choose as role models."

Tim McCarthy, a former secular disc jockey from Port Arthur, Texas, says of rock music, "People don't understand sometimes the power that a disc jockey has. This man can move people to shut up, to talk, to jump off buildings, to do anything, and just being there playing that music is promoting a bad lifestyle."

Even some of rock's most famous are willing to admit it's not good for them to be viewed as idols. Pete Townshend, former songwriter and vocalist for The Who, editorialized on the rock hero through a character in his book, *Horse's Neck*, a collection of short stories. "These dilettante pretenders are worshipped," declaims the character. "Stars are attributed with intelligence they don't have, beauty they haven't worked for, loyalty and love they are incapable of reciprocating, and strength they do not possess."[6]

---

[5]*Rolling Stone Interviews* (Vol. 1), p. 410.
[6]Pete Townshend, *Horse's Neck* (England: Houghton Mifflin).

Despite his insight, Townshend seems to have little concern for his idolizing fans. When 11 young people were trampled to death or asphyxiated outside one of his concerts, Townshend said of the incident, "We're not going to let a little thing like this stop us. . . . We're a rock 'n' roll band. You know we don't [expletive deleted] around worrying about 11 people dying."[7]

As a generation raised in the era of electronic entertainment, weaned on a steady diet of glitz, it's not difficult to understand why we are sucked into this antihero love and loyalty. We are a nation in which nearly every home possesses 2 televisions and 6 radios, where 81 percent have stereo systems and nearly 40 percent own video cassette recorders.

It is clear why we are drawn to that which is most glittering instead of that which is most enduring. As author Ralph Schoenstein admits, "Heroines like Marie Curie and Joan of Arc have been replaced by Marie Osmond and Joan Collins. . . . Americans today find less appeal in the right stuff than in the right fluff."[8]

This trend is sure to continue for some time to come. Rock music—dubbed a fad in the fifties—shows no sign of waning in popularity. Consequently, with little more than a well-planned media blitz, an androgenous boy named George can shake our culture, and a material girl named Madonna can affect the wardrobes (not to mention the moral values) of millions of idolizing Madonna-wanna-be's.

The Real Rock Hero

"Whether Christians like it or not," says author Calvin Miller, best known for his allegories *The Singer, The Song,* and *The Finale,* "rock is definitely going to mark the last half of the twentieth century with things that are going to be there for the next four or five centuries." That is an awesome thought—especially since today's rock music heroes seem to take their role-modeling so lightly, preferring instead to look out for their own interests.

---

[7] *Rolling Stone* (6/26/80), p. 38.
[8] Ralph Schoenstein, "My Turn," *Newsweek* (8/6/84), p. 9.

A genuine hero, on the other hand, is one who takes action in the face of danger for another's benefit. At the risk of sounding like a lead-in for a Marvel comic book, we contend a true hero looks for the common good despite personal sacrifice.

Of course, Jesus Christ gave us the best example of a real hero when He came to bridge the gap between us and God the Father. Jesus said He came so we could have life and "live it to the fullest" (John 10:10), and He died to prove He meant what He said. Now that's a real rock hero, a genuine role model!

He wasn't the type of person many of us parents might picture Him to be, however. He was no middle-class conservative with white collar and tastefully striped tie. He also wasn't as many young people perceive Him: a wimpy Clark Kent character, to which no one today could possibly relate. He was—and is—the ultimate hero: radical in style, without pretense or phoniness, sure of himself and His purpose, ready to die for those He loves, a real champion of what is right and true. He challenges us to be the same, to be champions for what's right and role models for each other.

But real heroes don't come from boxes of breakfast food. They don't come from the blusterings of mixed-up rock stars, either. It doesn't take anything extraordinary to be a hero—not with the Lord in you.

Frank E. Gaebelein, a theologian and connoisseur of the arts, described the kind of hero we all can be: " 'Jesus Christ laid down his life for us. And we ought to lay down our lives for our brothers.' . . . But what is it to lay down your life for your brothers or sisters? . . . It means caring more about people than dollars and things."[9]

That doesn't sound like the cheap philosophies of Pearcy, James or Crosby, does it? Instead, it sounds like being willing to stand for what's right.

Tim McCarthy, now a deejay for a Christian contemporary music radio station, says, "I don't care how much you don't want to hear it or believe it or do it, you've got to take a stand. It's

---

[9]Frank Gaebelein, *The Christian, The Arts, and Truth*, (Portland, Oreg.: Multnomah Press, 1985), p. 245.

true. And whether you realize it or not, you *are* taking a stand. If it's not for God, then you're taking a stand for the world and what it stands for. Maybe you aren't aware of it, but believe me, you're doing it."

"We need some heroes, for the Lord" sings the Christian group WhiteHeart. "We need some heroes, strong in the Word/ We need some brothers to carry the fight/We need some sisters with faith in what's right./We gotta stand up, who's gonna stand up?"

While being a hero may be a simple thing, we are not saying it's always the most popular position to be in. Christian performer Michael Sweet says, "A lot of people are afraid to stand up for something, even when they know it's right, and so they give in to peer pressure. But if you make sure you have God on your side, no one is big enough to put on boxing gloves and go into the ring with *Him*. And it's so encouraging to know you have someone there you can talk to at any time. Jesus is the ultimate friend who is always thinking about you, who always cares about you, who has His eye on you every moment. If you don't know Him, introduce yourself to Him, and once you do, make sure you don't walk out on that friend."

Sweet is right. With God on our side, we all can be winners. Then we can, as the Imperials sing, "Let the Wind Blow." Former member, Jim Murray explains: "Sometimes we feel insecure. Satan attacks us, but we need to know we've already overcome that. . . . It's already been done. No matter what comes—storm, wind, lightning, whatever—as long as you're founded in the Lord Jesus Christ—you can say, 'Let the wind blow. Me and the Lord are a majority!' "

Isn't it time to take a stand for the Lord, to put away the false answers mainstream rock music promotes and accept the challenge offered by *the* Rock—the one who gives life real meaning? Isn't it time to answer the call to be heroes for the Lord and—as Paul says in 2 Timothy—fight "the good fight"?

Being a hero often requires making changes, though. After all, when an athlete is about to fight a championship match or enter a grueling race, he doesn't surround himself with carousing companions, party all night, or fill his body with junk food and his mind with negative thoughts. If he wants to win—or even finish the race honorably—he trains diligently and envelops himself in positive people and power-filled thoughts. He takes care of himself inwardly and outwardly.

In the next chapter, we'll discuss some of the ways we all need to train if we are going to be heroes, and we'll decide if Christian rock music qualifies as a "hero sandwich" or merely junk food.

Chapter Four

Pop Music: Junk Food or Hero Sandwich?

We must be discerning to avoid being deceived. We need to know what we believe and why we believe it.

—*Campus Life,* music critic Jim Long

"Music is energy, just like food," according to Dr. Steve Halpern, a California composer and music-therapy researcher. "Having the right music around the house is as important as having the right food and the right vitamins."[1]

The late Frank E. Gaebelein, who fought zealously to revive Christian involvement in music and the arts, also spoke of music as food, but he warned against filling up on the junk-food variety: "If we feed our minds and spirits on garbage—and there's plenty of it around these days—that's bound to lead to decay and putridity within us."[2]

Junk-food music, it appears, is as bad for our spirits as empty calories are for our bodies. Listening to cheap music can eventually make us spiritually flabby, and spiritual flabbiness is not the stuff heroes are made of. "It's like cheesecake," says Christian entertainer David Meece. "An occasional piece of cheesecake now and then probably won't hurt you, but it won't make you healthy and you can't live off it."

We are what we listen to, it seems, as much as we are what

---

[1]*Prevention* (10/83), p. 63.
[2]Frank E. Gaebelein, *The Christian, the Arts, and Truth* (Portland, Oreg.: Multnomah Press, 1985), p. 102.

we eat. As the Christian rock group Petra sings, we are like "Computer Brains": "You must screen every entry made, the consequences must be weighed/The only way to security, is every thought in captivity./Computer brains, put garbage in/Computer brains, get garbage out."

Count It All Rubbish?

Gaebelein says musical junk food can actually rot the foundation of one's faith: "For young people to live day by day with . . . vulgar entertainment may tear down what they have heard in church and learned in Sunday school."[3] Despite its dangers, however, the garbage variety of secular rock music is most often promoted. *U.S. News & World Report* states: "According to a growing number of critics, irresponsible adults in the entertainment business are bedazzling the vulnerable young with a siren song of the darker sides of life. Violence, the occult, sadomasochism, rebellion, drug abuse, promiscuity and homosexuality are constant themes. . . . Video images are just as lurid—even though one quarter of the nationwide audience for MTV is under the age of 15."[4]

Though most secular rock music is not exactly hero-sandwich material, we must make one thing clear before we discuss healthful alternatives. While a complete ban would certainly spare us the effort of careful analysis, we are not suggesting all rock music is evil or that secular pop music should be indiscriminately tossed out with the trash. Granted, in anger at the garbage offered our youngsters, we may sometimes have wanted to scream, "Throw it all out!" That, however, would be super-spiritually throwing the baby out with the bath water.

Instead, we ought to use the judgment God has given us. In fact, Jesus, the ultimate truth, said He would send each believer "the Spirit of truth, whom the world cannot receive, because it neither sees him nor knows him" (John 14:17, RSV). Thus the Christian possesses what the world just doesn't have.

---

[3]Ibid., p. 57.
[4]*U.S. News & World Report* (10/28/85), p. 46.

Scripture also reveals, however, that God showers His blessings on both believers and unbelievers, the good and the bad alike. While Christians may have a corner on truth, we do not control the entire market—even the most ungodly person can speak wisdom. Therefore, though it may be easier to classify everything the world produces—rock music included—as immoral or wrong, but it's just not that simple.

Veteran performer in both secular and Christian music, Kerry Livgren, comments, "I like to listen to Wagner. I like to listen to Debussy. But both these men were incredible pagans. [They were] totally reprehensible characters, atheists, and yet their music is some of the most sublime I've ever heard. When I hear it, it lifts me out of myself and I praise God. The fact is, that music came from God, and when I hear it, I give praise and glory to God, even though those men hated God. You can't draw a line and say . . . listen to this, or don't listen to that. It's an area where you must, 'Let every man be convinced in his own mind.' "

Love Ditties vs. Wholesome Things

Martin Luther realized that many of the junk-food lyrics of his day were weakening young people's moral strength in much the same way as it does today. In his preface to the *Wittenberg Gesangbuch* of 1524, he said, "I wish that the young men might have something to rid them of their love ditties and wanton songs and might instead learn wholesome things and thus yield willingly to the good." In other words, Luther believed righteous living was becoming difficult for them because of the influence of cheap music.

But while he was aware of music's potential for both good and evil, Luther was also convinced of its importance. Therefore he said, "I am not of the opinion that all the arts shall be crushed to earth . . . as some bigoted persons pretend, but would willingly see them all, and especially music, servants of Him who gave and created them." Luther insisted the people of his time should put their musical tastes under Christ's lordship, seeking what Jesus would have them listening to. He hoped they would employ discernment instead of bigotry.

Let's be honest. Just as ungodly men such as Wagner and Debussy, in their day, could produce music reflecting God's character, even the most degenerate rock and roller is capable of writing or performing a song with truth and beauty. It does happen. For example, the infamous Doobie Brothers recorded "Jesus Is Just Alright With Me." Likewise, agnostics Andrew Lloyd Webber and Tim Rice composed the musical *Joseph and the Amazing Technicolor Dreamcoat.*

"Give Me a C, a Spiritual C!"

We also must remember, there is nothing magical about the words "secular" and "rock" that instantly turn what they touch to evil. Secular simply refers to that which is not sacred or religious, not bound by the laws of the church. Your checkbook is not sacred or religious, and is bound only by the laws of mathematics (and your bank). There is nothing evil about your checkbook, though it can be used for evil purposes. The same is true of secular music.

Furthermore, when we use the term secular in the context of this book, we don't mean to imply something evil. We are simply referring to music produced by mainstream artists and producers, as opposed to music produced specifically by Christian artists.

Likewise, when we say "rock" music we are referring to style of music, not the music's content. Perhaps rock is a difficult word for some to accept in connection with Christian music because the term was originally derived from a sexual slang term. It is unfortunate that this music style took its name from such a crude source. However, it would be difficult to use any other name and still be clearly understood. Others prefer terms such as Jesus music or contemporary Christian music (CCM), but rock is still the most universally understood term.

So whether we say "mainstream" or "secular," "contemporary" or "rock" is not important. What makes a particular piece of music evil is not its label. After all, we need to ask ourselves, does a musical scale differentiate between a secular C and a spiritual C? Can we find on a piano both an evil C and a righteous

C? Is there such a thing as a secular guitar and a Christian guitar?

Luther advises we throw preconceived ideas aside and learn how to discern. Of course, that's the tricky part. *Campus Life* music critic Harold Smith says, "In confronting rock's moral ambiguity, we must be 'as wise as serpents.' Our world view—if it is truly ours—*will* affect how we accept the offerings from the rock world—good and bad.

"Where we can be supportive—and thus be 'salt' and 'light'— let us be supportive. But where our understanding of Christ and his ways collide with the often perverse individualism of rock man and rock woman, then we must turn away."[5]

True wisdom comes in learning the difference, in learning how to be "in the world" but not "of it." It's a principle that has always challenged believers. But as Christian composer and writer John Fischer says, Scripture does not command us to "become a cultural ostrich." The answer, he insists, is to stop being passive listeners.[6] It's a real test of our faith and abilities, but the only way to honestly deal with rock music—and all the arts.

Christian Seal of Approval

We are not saying music must always be outwardly religious or stamped with an overt salvation message to be true or good. Neither must it bear some sort of "Christian Seal of Approval" to be acceptable or right. Sometimes we as Christians exhibit a sort of artistic secular phobia—a fear of secular artistic expression.

If we were to apply this standard to other fields, however, we would seek out only Christian electricians and Christian garbage collectors. We would buy Christian food at Christian grocery stores and cook it on Christian stoves. We would wear only Christian clothes and wash them in Christian laundry detergent.

Amy Grant's tour manager, Malcolm Greenwood, says, "For some reason we as Christians—and I'm throwing rocks at myself with this . . . have taken a music element and we have elevated

---

[5]Harold Smith, "On Record," *Campus Life* (12/85), p. 68.
[6]*Contemporary Christian* (1/85), p. 34.

it and put it on a pedestal. [We have said] that it can only be used to glorify God and if you're a Christian and you have a voice, then you can only sing Christian songs. I don't know why that has happened. They don't do the same thing with a plumber, a salesman, an auto mechanic or anything else."

This concept sounds ridiculous when applied to "everyday" occupations. Certainly, no one asked Paul if his tents were Christian. But in music and the other arts, many Christians seem to fear anything not linked directly to the cross.

We need to realize music gains validity when it is honest, in meaning and motive. We should thank God for the occasional honest love song, reflecting the blessing of choosing someone to cherish forever. We should rejoice when an artist—whether secular or Christian—is candid with kids about life's problems, and offers solutions. We should welcome lyrics from *anyone* willing to tell young people someone cares, thus giving them hope in the midst of trials. As Francis Schaeffer once said, "We must realize that art doesn't have to be a gospel tract to be right."[7]

Lest we get out of balance on this issue, another clarification is needed: Just as secular rock music isn't bad simply because it is secular, the opposite is also true—not every piece of artistic work labeled "Christian" is automatically right or true. Generally speaking, of course, contemporary Christian music fills a need for wholesome entertainment and edification, but not because secular music is all bad or Christian music is all good.

It's simply that if we are looking for the very best we should look in the most likely place. We can search in a restaurant's dumpster and eventually find something to eat; but it's silly to do so when abundant, nourishing food is right inside the restaurant door. Likewise, we aren't apt to find healthful food in a candy shop.

Nevertheless, a "Christian" song doesn't guarantee its worth or validity. We must use music—even Christian music—responsibly. After all, many cults use a Christian Bible, but distort its meaning, and the devil twists Scripture to suit his purposes when

---

[7]"The Battle for Our Culture," an Interview with Francis Schaeffer, *New Wine* (2/82), p. 7.

tempting us (cf. John 4:1–12). Likewise, Madonna wears cruci-
fixes and Prince babbles on about God in his music. Does that
make their music acceptable? Of course not. Symbols and labels
don't validate; meaning and motive validate.

All That Glitters

We live in an imperfect world, and much of what we produce
bears the marks of our imperfection. It may look good or sound
good, but in reality be inaccurate, empty or worthless. Our world
is like a jewelry store window which displays both cheap trinkets
and precious jewels, but some prankster has crept in and ex-
changed some of the price tags. We have some glittering junk
jewelry bearing high prices, while many items of real quality
appear to be nearly worthless.

"This means," says Gaebelein, "that Christian artists and all
of us for whom the arts are an essential part of life and culture
must constantly be keeping our eyes open to the marks of the
fall."[8] We need to be aware that just as secular music can give us
cheap or immoral solutions to our problems, Christian music can
sometimes preach a cheap gospel, or even worse, be down right
wrong.

If we are not going to be duped into taking home this junk
jewelry, we have to know the difference. As Christian singer Amy
Grant warns in song, "Everyone will have their words to say/Find
the word to help you find your way/You've got to know who to,
who not to listen to."

Rather than blindly following what others tell us, God desires
that we be skilled discerners of the good and the bad, not only
in music, but in every area of our lives. Though we hope we're
offering some good ideas in this book, we wouldn't want anyone
thoughtlessly to accept our viewpoint. Using prayerful discernment we all need to judge the messages in our music. Christian
new-wave artist Steve Crumbacher urges young people to seek
truth and question their musical choices: "The main thing I want
people to do is to look into things themselves—not to just be led

---

[8]Gaebelein, op. cit., p. 75.

along constantly by other people. . . . I think the ones that ask questions of themselves and then go and look for the answers—with God's help—are the stronger ones."

God also desires we admit when music is personally inappropriate. He wants each of us to seek out, discover and choose the very best for us, understanding that (in the arts) what is appropriate for one person may not always be right for another. Themes of some music, for instance, might be too sophisticated for younger listeners, and could lead to misunderstandings.

The most important question to answer, then, is not a question of secular or Christian music. It is, as in every area of life, *what does God want for me?*

The answer to this question will be different for each one of us. It will be based on a variety of factors, including age, life experiences, and maturity. After all, we each need nourishing food, but even the best of foods are not appropriate for everyone. A newborn doesn't have teeth to handle solid food. Likewise, orange juice may be packed with health-giving vitamins but is poison to someone allergic to it. In the same way, each of us Christians is running the same spiritual race, but our training tables are set differently. Therefore, we each need to check our musical menus with the Lord. And to do that we need some guidelines—some rules to follow.

In the next few chapters, we'll look at some of those rules for choosing music which is personally right, and we will apply those rules specifically to Christian rock music by looking at the four basics: the lyrics, the lifestyles, the goals and the graphics.

Chapter Five

The Shalts and Shalt Nots of Music

We need honest songs about hope in the midst of trials. We need songs about real temptations we go through. We must not make sin look like fun, but by being transparent with our lyrics, people can learn that temptation, problems and suffering are common to all of us—and that Jesus is still the answer.

—*Melody Green*

Rock music, which fuels a 4.3-billion-dollar-a-year recording industry, is a powerful, sometimes malevolent, persuader. John Michael Talbot, whose records and songbooks have sold more than a million copies, says, "Music has incredible power. Wrongly used, it can stir our darkest inner impulses—lust and anger and despair. But Christian music, music that truly speaks about the Lord and to the Lord, draws upon that great power to stir our hearts in their longing for God."[1]

When Solomon evoked God's presence to fill the temple, he used the great spiritual power of music. When David was commanded to soothe King Saul's demonic depression, he utilized music's great psychological power (a practice still applied today, especially in dental offices!). Likewise, music's emotional power instilled courage in fighting men from the days of Moses and Joshua until today.

If Christian music does, as Talbot says, powerfully stir our hearts toward God, why can we not simply list a Christian Top

---

[1] John Michael Talbot, "Music's Mysterious Power," *Charisma* (2/86), p. 22.

40? One reason is that music affects us individually.

As critic Harold C. Goddard says, "There is no mystery in a looking glass until someone looks into it. Then though it remains the same glass, it presents a different face to each man who holds it in front of him. The same is true of a work of art. It has no proper existence as art until someone is reflected in it—and no two will ever be reflected in the same way."[2] Since no two people will view a piece of music the same way, it is impossible for us to simply produce an "approved" list of either tunes or artists. As the saying goes, "Different strokes for different folks."

Of course, it would be an easy task to discern if some music were intrinsically evil and other music were naturally good. Then we could just eliminate the evil sounds or beat or noise level and the problem would dissolve. However, that would, as John Murray says, place the responsibility for wrong "at the door of things rather than at man's heart."[3] Besides, who would decide which sounds are evil? Who would say which sound is too noisy and which beat is too fast? We will discuss this in depth later, but as author and sociologist Tony Compolo puts it, "Some of the music popular among youth today within the realm of Christian music is good and some of it is bad. The issue does not particularly relate to the type of music as much as to what is communicated and expressed in the music."[4] And, we might add, to whom it is communicated. It's not just the heart of the singer or songwriter that needs examination, but also the heart of the listener.

Furthermore, we must be realistic. We are all human beings and we all make mistakes. Though we wish it weren't so, some Christian artists—just as Christians in any walk of life—have experienced marital difficulties, even substance abuse problems. Some have produced faulty doctrine or strayed off the narrow road in other ways.

If we were to draw up a list of "right-on" artists today, it's likely at least one of them would have developed problems, making it necessary to take him off the list before this book even goes to press.

---

[2]Harold G. Goddard, *The Meaning of Shakespeare* (New York, 1951), p. 331.
[3]*Moody Monthly* (9/85), p. 34.
[4]*Christian Life* (12/85), p. 14.

It's not that musical performers are a particularly sinful lot—but that they are human. It's not that they participate in a wretched, sin-filled occupation—but there are pitfalls. Even the most conservative, puritanical places have harbored perversion and sin. We are all products of the fall, and a list of any group—pipefitters, painters or pastors—would likely suffer the same problem. Discernment must therefore be an ongoing process. That's why we have chosen not to endorse particular artists or certain styles of music, but to give criteria by which a person can judge music individually.

The Ten Commandments of Music

Well-known speaker and writer Steve Clark asserts Scripture is the rule against which everything else has to be tested. "We should confront our thinking with the Scripture regularly. . . . We should learn to let God's word override our natural or secular conclusions."[5] Likewise, John Wesley once boasted, "I am a Bible bigot. I follow it in all things, both great and small." Though each situation and person may be different, Scripture is constant. That's why God's Word is the premier personal yardstick to use in every area of our lives, including our music.

But does the Bible mention music? Definitely. In fact, music, musicians and musical instruments are mentioned in the Bible over 800 times! One of our favorite passages on the subject, Colossians 3:15–17, not only discusses music but gives some general rules by which we can establish God's will for us concerning it:

> The peace that Christ gives is to guide you in the decisions you make; for it is to this peace that God has called you together in the one body. And be thankful. Christ's message in all its richness must live in your hearts. Teach and instruct one another with all wisdom. Sing psalms, hymns, and sacred songs; sing to God with thanksgiving in your hearts. Everything you do or say, then, should be done in the name of the Lord Jesus, as you give thanks through him to God the Father. (GNB)

Using this scripture passage as a guideline, let's list some

---

[5]Steve Clark, *Knowing God's Will* (Ann Arbor, Mich.: Word of Life, 1974), p. 19.

"shalts" and "shalt nots" for music:

1. *Your music shall not destroy peacefulness in your heart.*

Peace—which Webster's describes as an undisturbed state of mind—is a quality of life promoted throughout the Bible. It is impossible to achieve, however, without God's presence. It is also one of the first fruits of the Spirit to disappear when we are out of God's perfect will or in spiritual danger. That makes peace—or the lack of it—a good indicator of the type of music to which we should listen.

If we experience a lack of peace—a sense of uneasiness within or a lack of harmony without—during or after listening to a certain style of music or the works of a particular group, then perhaps God is saying that specific music is not appropriate or healthy for us, or at least not presently.

It may seem like a little thing—why worry if you feel a little uneasy? What harm can it do? But God knows our weaknesses and He gave us a conscience to help guide us. As Christian singer/ songwriter Steve Camp sings, the absence of peace is a sign we're on shaky ground: "Looks like the boy's in trouble again/Living much too close to the edge of sin/Now he finds himself where he should not have been/Oh God, why is Your peace so hard to find?"

God makes His peace "hard to find" as a danger signal for our spiritual well-being, just as pain is a danger signal for our physical health. He knows the areas where we are vulnerable. He knows weaknesses most likely to cause us to fall, and He warns us by withdrawing His peace. If you feel disquieted by certain music, simply get rid of it. It's obviously not right for you.

2. *Your music shall not cause disunity in the body.*

A noted jazz musician, Ira Gitler, once said, "Above all other considerations, rock is definitely the music of today's youth and its importance is more social than musical. . . . It sets them apart from the values and attitudes of the adult, establishment world in a more emphatically schismatic manner than ever before."[6]

---

[6]*Bell Telephone* (1–2/70), as quoted in *Pop Goes the Gospel,* John Blanchard with Peter Anderson and Derek Cleave (England: Evangelical Press, 1983), p. 125.

It's true. Rock music is a powerful medium, affecting every segment of society. As such, it has the potential to cause division, especially between kids and their parents, between youth groups and their pastors, but unity—especially within the family of God—is too important to let music get in the way.

Larry Weber, of the unique Christian group Weber and the Buzztones, stresses, "My big message, the thing I really try to press home to people, is that it's not the bands that are going to change America. The thing we try to stress is the family. . . . That is where my heart really is. . . . I enjoy playing music a lot, but music is certainly at the bottom of the totem pole."

If you are a young person, you need to honestly ask yourself what position music has taken in your life. Have your parents or pastor voiced a concern that music occupies too much of your time? Do they disagree with your choices? Has your favorite music caused problems between you and your parents? Do you listen, in rebellion, to music they have forbidden?

If so, God has a strong message for you—but not without a terrific promise: "My son, hear the instruction of your father, and do not forsake the law of your mother; For they will be graceful ornaments on your head, and chains about your neck" (Prov. 1:8–9, NKJV).

Just as jewelry makes the wearer look good, respecting the wishes of those in authority over you makes you look good—not only to your parents, or to God, but to everyone!

Furthermore, you have an obligation to "obey your parents in the Lord," as Paul says. It might be hard, but as Christian new-wave-cum-wit artist Steve Taylor puts it, we show our love for God by our obedience. "That's what love for God means—being obedient. The obedience factor is very important, and the more we know about the Bible, the more we know what God expects of us. . . ."[7]

If your parents or pastor are convinced your rock music is harming you—even if it is Christian rock—do your best to live by their rules. You'll never be sorry.

If you are a parent or pastor, be assured we fully understand

---

[7]Jon Trott, "Steve Taylor," *Cornerstone* (Vol. 12: Issue 66), p. 41.

your doubts and concerns about Christian rock. We have also experienced some of the same feelings. But we hope this book will help both you and your young people to better understand the proper criteria used to judge music. We trust you will resist the temptation to brand music sinful because of its rhythm or noise level, and instead take time to think about the practical and spiritual principles offered here. Though all music requires personal discernment, we have observed parents needlessly frustrating their children and actually undermining their own authority by indiscriminately banning Christian rock's "joyful noise." As parents, we must remember that when Paul reminded children to obey their parents, he also strongly cautioned, "Fathers, do not provoke your children to wrath, but bring them up in the training and admonition of the Lord" (Eph. 6:4, NKJV).

Of this warning, Edith Schaeffer comments, "There needs to be time for careful examination day by day as to what you might be doing to exasperate your children and turn them away from both you and the Lord, rather than giving them excitement and interest in pursuing truth."[8]

In wisdom and love, then, we should try to understand music's appeal to young people, and work together with our children to find music appropriate to their age and level of maturity.

We hope both adults and teens will strive to keep music in perspective and not allow it to cause family division. As the Christian group Petra sings, we need to stand firm against Satan who enjoys seeing us tangled in disputes: "He'll catch your eye with some cheap disguise/Or innocent distraction/Then he'll infiltrate the ranks/And split you into factions." By putting love, understanding and a firm commitment to communication before our personal music preferences, however, we can outsmart Satan and keep harmony in the home.

3. *Your music shall not cause ungratefulness.*

Our society faces many problems—drugs, sexual pressures, threats of war, family breakdowns, physical and sexual abuse— and Christians are no exception. As pastor-singer Glenn Kaiser

---

[8]Edith Schaeffer, *Common Sense Christian Living* (Nashville, Tenn.: Thomas Nelson, 1983), p. 127.

of Rez Band puts it, "We try to relate to hurts on a human level. Christians still have zits. Christians get flat tires. They get cancer and die."[9] Kaiser is talking about being real, about being honest. It's important we don't pretend troubles disappear when we accept Jesus; and an honest musical appraisal of problems, faults or human issues can lead to thoughtful self-searching and positive change.

On the other hand, if the heart attitude of either the artist or the listener is negative or angry, unrest and rebellion are often the only result. Ulfe Christiansson, front man for the Swedish Christian rock band Jerusalem, says, "You can find a lot of questions but you also need to have the answers. Most Christians today know a lot of things that are wrong, but we also need to know the answer; and the answer is a spiritual answer, an answer about our hearts."

We're not saying every song needs to be a hearts-and-flowers praise song, or to present all the answers to life's complex problems. If your music asks questions about life, however, it should always point you *toward* the answers. As Christian rocker Kenny Marks maintains, "In any large group of people (like the folks I sing to every night) almost every human condition is represented. There are winners, losers, lovers, haters, givers, takers, people who feel hopeful and those who have no hope at all. . . . But the key is, how does Christ come in and affect these people?"

Melody Green, whose late husband Keith was involved in Jesus music from the early sixties, also believes music should point toward the answer: "Every song need not have a salvation message, but music needs to be transparent, to be honest. We need honest songs about hope in the midst of trials. We need songs about real temptations we go through. We must not make sin look like fun, but by being real with our lyrics, people can learn that temptation, problems and suffering are common to all of us—and that Jesus is still the answer."

We also need to learn the difference between satire and sarcasm—constructive criticism versus destructive negativism—in both our music and in our personal response to it. As Steve

---

[9]"The New Christian Minstrels," *Newsweek* (8/19/85), p. 70.

Taylor notes, "To me much of the book of Proverbs is satirical. . . . Yet its purpose obviously is not to tear down but to change things."[10]

A sarcastic, critical attitude, on the other hand, is often destructive and leaves the listener feeling ungrateful or angry. Explains Taylor, "There had been different people in Christian music who were writing songs about the church with a chip on their shoulders. They weren't really involved in the church the way they should have been. Maybe they had a bad experience with the church, or something like that . . . sort of like the theology student who doesn't go to church. Who needs that?

"My background is growing up in the church. My dad is a pastor. I never went through a big stage of rebellion. I never got to a place where I ditched the church because I got angry. . . . I just felt it was better for an insider, who loves the church and wants to see the church conform to the image of Christ, to write songs than for someone with a chip on their shoulder to write songs because they're angry."

Taylor's heart attitude seems to be a positive one, and his songs cleverly challenge. However, each of us must also look at our own response to this style of music and make certain the music does not affect us negatively. If you find yourself feeling too judgmental, critical, or cynical, perhaps your musical menu needs refocusing toward more positive selections.

4. *Your music shall not disagree with the Word of God.*

We need to be watchful for false doctrine couched in catchy tunes. It can fill our heads with useless garbage, and even lead us astray. Andrew Fletcher, a 19th-century Scottish politician, once said, "Let me write the ballads of a nation and I care not who may write its laws." And this was before the day of the Walkman! How much more important today that our music be checked against God's Word and based on His laws. James 3:1 says, "Let not many of you become teachers," because they will be "judged with greater strictness" (RSV). Music teaches and music greatly impacts people; therefore, we must make certain our music is theologically correct.

---

[10]Jon Trott, Ibid.

The vivacious Annie Herring, lead singer for The Second Chapter of Acts, says she always checks out her lyrics with Scripture: "There are so many ways to use [music] to express yourself. . . . You really have to 'press in' to know what He wants for us so that the music isn't just our opinion, but the heart of God."

Likewise, long-time Christian folksinger Barry McGuire says he strives to present the truth of the gospel in his music: "I am trying to catch songs that make such a statement of truth that everybody who hears it will totally realize that they have just heard the truth."[11]

Unfortunately, not every artist works so hard to ensure his lyrics are scripturally accurate. Wes Yoder, who has participated in Jesus music in one way or another since its inception, and who now represents a number of prominent Christian artists, says of Christian rock, "Thousands and thousands of people have been won to the Lord through Christian music, and thousands and thousands of Christians have been strengthened in their faith through it.

"I'm concerned though, about the drift that I'm seeing of people writing songs just to get hits, and they are accommodating Biblical lyrics to finding a better rhyme and they're saying things that just should never have been said. . . . I don't mean that in the worst sense, but it seems most Christian artists are not students of the Word of God. They are students of how to have a hit record, how to get the best publishing deal, but they are not also students of the Word of God, which has got to be central to all that."

5. *Your music shall not be sordid and cheap.*

If pop music has one downfall, it is its penchant for instant answers and cheap philosophy. Calvin Miller, an author and pastor, cautions that we can be so slick in our presentation of music that the message becomes nothing but glitter in the process: "I still think when you become so closely identified with all the methods and sounds of culture, you lose that distinction that used to say, 'We are the people of God.' We must be sure that the difference is there—words like sacrifice, commitment, taking up

---

[11]*The Best of Contemporary Christian Music* 1979–1980, p. 42.

your cross daily—words that are 'scare clauses' to the world. If that's well-defined then the nature of our promotions, be it rock or whatever, can largely be a matter of taste."

Of course, not every song we enjoy needs to extoll the virtues of the cross, but we should constantly search for quality in our music, for the best. Artist Keith Green once wrote, "Jesus doesn't want us to be as good as the world, He wants us to be better! And that doesn't mean excelling them in sound, style, or talent—it means surpassing them in value. . . ."[12]

We think Christian music should surpass the world's product in sound, style, and especially in *value*. As Rez Band sings, "Who needs . . . plastic music, plastic food/Cellophane tunes for that/ Synthetic mood/. . . What this world needs/ Is music that feeds/ Not Elevator Muzik." In other words, who needs music about saving our souls if that music doesn't provide the real meat of the gospel. None of us can survive on a starvation diet of "Jesus loves me, He set me free, la-di-da-dee-dee-dee."

Petite Wendi Kaiser, the group's gravel-voiced, power-packed vocalist adds, "We don't preach an easy gospel. We don't say, 'Get saved and everything will be fine.' My husband believes firmly there is no crown without the cross. You must *repent* and believe; you can't just believe. Repentance is absolutely crucial to your Christian walk. Or else it's just a cheap gospel."

Unfortunately, however, it is this cheap gospel that often gets set to music. Frankly, there seems to be a very disturbing trend of artists seeking to be accepted by the world, and applying not just the world's methods, but the world's standards to Christian music.

It is a sad picture—all the more so when we think of the value of the public platform a Christian artist possesses. As musician/ writer John Fischer says, losing integrity in order to win the world makes us double losers—with God and man: "It would be tragic indeed to give up the one thing we possess that the world can recognize—something to believe in, something to stand for, something to live for, and something to die for."[13]

---

[12]"Can God Use Rock Music?", Keith Green, © 1982, *Pretty Good Printing* (Last Days Ministries, Box 40, Lindale, TX 75771).

[13]John Fischer, "Sound Advice," *Contemporary Christian* (1/86), p. 46.

6. *Your music shall not destroy hope in your heart.*

So much of today's pop music—including some contemporary Christian music—is dark music, devoid of hope. We are convinced—as are many psychology experts—that the despair preached through much of today's "realistic" music is producing a sickness of heart, which is a factor in a rising epidemic of teenage suicide. While music can simply list problems, it also must supply answers. If a song speaks of darkness, it must point to the Light; if it speaks of hurt, it must provide healing.

We don't mean to suggest all Christian artists become Pollyannish in their approach to lyrics, but we do see a need for more encouragement through music. Christian artist Angie Lewis, for example, sings realistically about pain in her hit single, "Silent Weeper," but she also says Jesus is there in the midst of sorrow. "I want people to know that I am just as human as they are. I hurt just like they do. I'm confused just like they are," she explains. "But in my music, I want them to know where I go and where they need to go to find the answers."

Likewise, Mark Gersmehl, of the lyrically and musically intense group WhiteHeart, tells his concert fans, "I don't know why you came here tonight. Maybe some of you have something heavy tugging at your heartstrings. . . . But there is a place you can go where you will always be loved back. When you're feeling so down that all you can find is the bottom of your heart, 'turn the page' of your life and look to the Lord Jesus Christ because He says to you, 'Come unto me all you who are weary and heavy laden, come to Me, and I'm going to give you rest. . . . I will not leave you desolate.' "

That kind of encouragement supplies realistic answers to those relating to the problems presented in a particular tune. While we don't want to look at life through rose-colored glasses (or stained-glass windows), we do need to declare war on discouragement in all forms. Satan will try to use anything—our music included—to discourage us and get us to renounce Christ. That's his ultimate goal. We therefore must be certain our music has the opposite goal: to—as Annie Herring says—"let people know the Lord's a redeemer, to provide hope to bruised people, to see people set free."

7. *Your music shall have lasting value.*

Though at one time we thought artists who simply entertained were not serving Christ, we have changed our minds.
We're now convinced there is a place for pure entertainment. As
the old adage goes, "All work and no play makes Jack a dull boy."
Don Finto, pastor of the Belmont Church in Nashville, Tenn.,
whose congregation includes Christian performers such as Amy
Grant, Michael W. Smith, Rob Frazier and Gary Paxton, insists,
"I really agree with Amy that part of their ministry is to put on
a good show, because kids need good shows. They need good
clean places to go."

We now believe the entertainment available through Christian rock music can provide vibrant memories for our youth. It
can help nurture an appreciation for God-given gifts of beauty,
creativity and music. The challenge is to strike a good balance
between musical entertainment and other priorities, and to make
certain we purchase something of value with our time and
money.

Dallas Holm tells us, "We are the most entertained society in
the world, and our lives are so cluttered with meaningless, worthless things. People just indulge in so much of no value."[14] Holm
is right. Americans spend 300 billion dollars a year on leisure
activities, and rock music claims a large chunk of that market.
Sales of records and tapes have soared to the highest levels in
history, thanks to the teenage market.

While it's fine to have fun, we do need to honestly appraise
our leisure time activities. Just as in Scripture we see Jesus often
chose between one good thing and another, we need to do some
thinking and choosing.

We need to ask ourselves: What is God's purpose for my time
and money? If I want to be a Christian hero, what should my
priorities be? It takes courage and boldness to be a hero, and
these come only from taking time to cultivate a relationship with
the Lord. As Melody Green says, "Music is not a substitute for
time with God, even worship music."

We must be sure we keep music—whatever kind it is—in its

---

[14]Foster Braun, "Dallas Holm and Praise," *Windstorm* (7–8/83), p. 28.

proper place. Remember, God didn't say, "Thou shalt have no other *bad* gods before me"; He simply said "gods." Period. And anything that takes God's place in our hearts is another god.

Furthermore, we should be certain our music teaches us something worthwhile—that it has what the publishing industry labels "take away" value. For, as the late arts scholar Frank Gaebelein once said, "Everyone needs recreation, but it is the quality of our recreation that reveals who we are."[15]

George Frederic Handel, who was a Christian as well as a musician, was concerned that his audiences received something of quality from his oratorios: "I should be sorry if I only entertained them," he said. "I wished to make them better."[16] This is the element we need to search for in our music. It should make us a better person, give us some training, information, or inspiration we can use to enhance our daily lives or personal walk with the Lord.

When asked by *Charisma* magazine what she thought of Christian music being used as a means of entertainment rather than for worship and ministry, many-time Dove Award winner Sandi Patti said, "I think there can be a balance. I want people to laugh and have a good time at my concerts, yet I want them to take home more than that. . . . I want some of the things we share to mean just as much the next morning; I don't want it limited to a couple of hours of a good time together."[17]

8. *Your music shall communicate knowledge.*

There is a saying that knowledge is power. Knowledge is a powerful weapon, but for the Christian, the most powerful is personal knowledge of God. By that, we don't mean knowing *about* God, but knowing God as a person and a friend. How well do you really know God? Do you know Him well enough to be convinced of His love for you even during tough times? It's very important that you do. In fact, it's a matter of life and death, as God reveals while grieving over His nation: "My people are destroyed from lack of knowledge" (Hosea 4:6, NIV).

---

[15] Frank Gaebelein, op. cit., p. 254.
[16] Curtis Forman, "Hallelujah!", *New Wine* (2/82), p. 10.
[17] *Charisma* (2/86), p. 42.

In Jeremiah's time, when God foretold Israel's destruction, He said it was due to the people's lack of knowledge. "My people are fools; they do not know me. They are senseless children; they have no understanding. They are skilled in doing evil; they know not how to do good" (Jer. 4:22, NIV). The people in Jeremiah's day hadn't taken time to know God, and they suffered for it. We can imagine them—people who, just as we, got busy and distracted by the world. They became token believers whose silly notions about who God is weren't enough to save them when the going got rough. These people were also a musical culture. Many of the important events in their lives revolved around music. It's safe to assume their music influenced their lack of knowledge of God and His ways, since throughout history, musicians have been influential cultural leaders. We can picture their musicians creating cute little ditties to give their audiences warm fuzzies about God, but no true knowledge.

Unfortunately, that description also fits some contemporary Christian music—shallow music that creates false images of God. We, however, want to listen to—as the advertising jingle says— "the real thing."

Veteran Christian singer and composer, Scott Wesley Brown, says, "I really get excited when I hear a song that shows me honesty, and it's not just a 'rah-rah Jesus' line put together that's got all the hip new licks on it."[18] We may all need to hear Oh-how-wonderful-it-is-to-be-saved music once in a while, but our music should both grow with us and help us to grow.

We need to be told God loves us and that Jesus is coming again. But that can be said only so many ways before it becomes unchallenging or repetitious, and even misleading. There comes a time when we need to be challenged, as Christians, to grow up and face the real world and its many problems. Otherwise, we may become, as Amy Grant sings, ". . . a fat little baby/He wants his bottle and he don't mean maybe/He's sampled solid food but once or twice/But he says doctrine leaves him cold as ice."

Music that helps us do that must go beyond beatitudes and platitudes. It has to, in some way, reflect God's character, or com-

---

[18]Jon Trott, "Interviews," *Cornerstone* (Vol. 10: Issue 54), p. 39.

municate godly truths, or promote an understanding of God's purpose for our lives. It may be lighthearted, but it still must have substance.

"There are so many people who are spiritually lax," says vocalist Ron Collins of the relative new-comers to Christian music, Twenty Twenty. "We see it in churches wherever we go—young people who call themselves Christians just because they go to church, yet they're really not living it. The main thing that we're trying to get across is that if you're not living it day to day, you need to be more Christlike."

Let's seek content in our music that will help us all become more Christlike. Let's demand substance such as Christian singer and songwriter Steve Camp describes when he reveals, "My songs have to touch slices of ordinary life and experiences in order to relate to Christ. . . . The guitar playing is great, good drum licks are fine . . . but if you have not taken time to get to know the Lord in a way that can really make a difference, it doesn't matter."[19]

9. *Your music shall contain wisdom.*

According to English singer and songwriter Garth Hewitt, no one is brought up in a vacuum; we are constantly learning *something*: "Influences come in all the time to our brains, but sadly, most people are like driftwood in the stream." If we don't want to bob around like driftwood, we need a firm anchor, we need wisdom.

Unfortunately, trivia rather than wisdom is the hot commodity in our culture. Trivia games grace our coffee tables, and trivial tunes play on our tape decks. While trivia is fun, and knowing who held the 1963 World Rollerskating Championship title may be interesting, we can't get to heaven on rollerskates.

Likewise, if music fills our leisure hours, we must continually question what it teaches—not simply is it good or bad, but is it wisdom or trivia? Food for thought or fluff? Worthwhile or a waste of time?

The Bible tells us the story of Jesus' visit to the home of His three friends, Lazarus, Mary and Martha (Luke 10:38–42).

---

[19]*MusicLine* (7/85), as reprinted in *New Christian Media* (11–12/85), pp. 32–33.

Upon Jesus' arrival, Martha immediately began bustling about, engrossed in trivial preparations for a meal with her honored guest. Meanwhile, Mary sat at Jesus' feet, absorbing His wisdom. When Martha realized Mary was not helping her, she demanded Jesus reprimand Mary. On the contrary, Jesus commended Mary for choosing the better thing.

In the same way, we need to make sure neither trivial matters of life nor trivial music consume our time and energies. As Christian entertainer Steve Taylor warns both his fans and his fellow songwriters, "Life's too short for small talk/So don't be talking trivia now./Excess baggage fills this plane/There's more than we should ever allow."

Life is "too short," and time seems to fly away. The Bible says our days our short as "an evening shadow," and the psalmist prays, "Teach us how short our life is, so that we may become wise" (Ps. 90:12, GNB).

Proverbs goes even further, urging young people, "Get wisdom; get insight. Do not forsake her and she will keep you; love her, and she will guard you" (Prov. 4:5, 6, RSV). A far cry from trivial pursuits, it's the pursuit of wisdom.

10. *Your music shall be sung in the name of the Lord.*

Often in advertising a prominent public figure or celebrity will lend his name to a product. And so, we have Cheryl Tiegs clothing, Arnie Palmer golf clubs, even Billy Beer! Of course, we all know abuses—Elvis Presley's promoter, Col. Parker, was so liberal with the star's name, he crassly authorized the printing of both "I love Elvis" and "I hate Elvis" buttons and bumper stickers. Lending one's name to a product, however, usually ensures a measure of quality and credibility.

Imagine if your name were used to endorse a product; you would want that product to be the very best. In the same way, because Christian contemporary music bears Christ's name, it should also bear the marks of His character. It should have quality and credibility. It should be the very best.

Britian's Christian music critic John Blanchard says Christian music "should be like God. It should reflect him, magnify him;

it should communicate something of God's character. Does it do this?"[20]

Based on this "musical shalt," you may be tempted to disqualify rock music, concluding nothing so loud and beat-happy could be sung "in the name of the Lord." While we once were tempted to think the same, we now conclude rhythm, style and volume are largely a matter of taste. And to be honest, many Christians, as Gaebelein has said, "attend with clear conscience performances labeled sacred concerts in which a good deal of third-rate sentimental music has been baptised, as it were, by association with Christian verse; or in which tawdry, tasteless hymn arrangements, false to any real musical integrity, are deemed religious."[21] Furthermore, many of these same people categorically condemn music in the contemporary vein, even when it's of the highest quality.

Music need not be hymn-like in order to point to God. It doesn't need to be sentimental "worship" music in order to be sung to the Creator of music. Likewise, a song which does not mention Jesus by name may bring glory to God and be sung "in the name of the Lord."

What, then, gives any music this godly "seal of approval"? How can we tell if Jesus is pleased to endorse a musical product? One way to test for this quality is to ask: If Jesus listened to this song, would He enjoy it? (Not because of His musical preferences, but because it is presented truthfully and performed artfully.) Does it avoid cheap answers? Does it seem sincere or does it feel contrived? In short, is it well done?

There is a sense in which all good music is a celebration of God. Therefore, if we can answer yes to these questions, then no matter what the key, tone, style, beat or subject, it probably passes God's inspection. It can be sung in God's name and He will be pleased.

---

[20]*Pop Goes the Gospel*, John Blanchard with Peter Anderson and Derek Cleave (England: Evangelical Press, 1983), p. 133.
[21]Frank E. Gaebelein, op. cit., pp. 165–166.

Part Two

Rating Christian Rock

It's important when we listen to music that we don't take it hook, line and sinker, but judge it.

—Rick Cua

In many Christian circles the beat, along with any other "worldly" properties is often grounds for instant condemnation of a tune. In fact, Steven Wyer, President of Sunbelt Management Group, who represents such Christian artists as Steve Camp, Rob Frazier and Rick Cua, recalls, "I had a pastor come up to me at our concert and inform me that our performance was really out in left field because we used green lights—and green lights were of the devil! I mean, if the color green is of the devil, then God must have been really confused when he made trees and grass! Where do these people get these ideas? What kind of judgment is that?"

At times, any one of us might question certain aspects of a concert or a particular style of music. And a somewhat skeptical attitude can help in discerning if a certain artist or style is right for us. However, we must remember to weed out responses based on culture, or discrediting what seems strange or different to us. We need not force ourselves to listen to music we don't like, but neither should we summarily condemn it.

As strange as some musical sounds and styles—or the color of stage lights—might seem to us, they are not evil merely because we don't appreciate them. Likewise, those same sounds and sights are not good simply because we find them personally appealing. Rating rock music means going *beyond* the beat or the sound—no matter whether the music is secular or Christian—and judging instead the lyrics and lifestyles, the goals and the graphics.

Chapter Six

Lyrics

Why can't we take that same powerful force—music—put positive lyrics to it and begin shaping values that way?

—Sandi Patti

Decidedly, the most important of the four criteria for judging music is the lyrics, the words, as borne out by the Psalms that King David wrote thousands of years ago. While we do not know the melodies to which they were set, the words are still alive and fresh. Obviously, David understood the power of words.

"The living word awakened my soul, gave it light, hope, joy, set it free," Helen Keller testified in her autobiography. And since Christianity is a belief system formed on "the Word" (Jesus is the Word "made flesh"—John 1:14), lyrics in Christian music, both traditional and contemporary, can transmit His life-transforming power. However, lyrics can also be cheap or dangerous— "Words can thrill or chill you/ Words can fill or kill you," sings Second Chapter of Acts. Christian entertainer Rick Cua, who formerly played with the mainstream hard rock band the Outlaws, solemnly warns, "Pop or gospel or country or jazz or classical or Christian—there's good and there's bad—and we have to listen to the lyrics." It's up to us, then, to discern rather than passively listen. Lyricist and Christian pop-rocker Pete Carlson adds, "You have to have discernment in Christian music as well [as mainstream]. . . . It's important when we listen to music that we don't take it hook, line and sinker, but we judge it."

Solo artist David Meece agrees: "Basically you have to focus on the lyrics, and what the song is saying. That is my criteria to decide whether the song is right or wrong. It has nothing to do with the music style. It has to do with the lyrics. What is the song saying? What are the words saying? As Christians, we can objectively judge it from that standpoint."

How can we be confident of deciding rightly? Cua assures, "The Holy Spirit will help us to discern . . . if we pray for discernment. It's . . . not a gift only to a few. We all have the Holy Spirit when we accept the Lord, and we can say, 'Lord, show me, help me, teach me how to discern. The basic right from wrong is obvious, but if there's more, Lord, let me tune into it.' "

Cua, a father of two teenage girls, insists parents should teach their kids how to discern in matters that aren't obviously right or wrong. "Don't say, 'It's wrong. Period.' Say, 'Look at this; this is what God says. Pray about it. What do you think?' Help them. Don't leave them totally in the dark, but don't answer all their questions for them either. That would be like a kid coming home with homework and a parent doing it. We all have homework to do; the Lord gives us homework to do and we need to learn on our own."

Our "homework", then, is to discover what the lyrics say, what values and ideas they teach. As documented in *Why Knock Rock?*, the general trend in secular music, rock or otherwise, is away from God, promoting ideas which oppose Judeo-Christian values. Entertainment-media expert Bill Huie observes: "The initial power and influence of the rock era was the medium itself. . . . The message in the beginning was very simple. Sex, good times, and teenage rebellion against parental control. But as the movement progressed and the fun 50s turned into the turbulence and insecurity of the 60s, the message began to change to more important matters."[1]

That change eventually resulted in messages which address our cultural values in six specific areas: (1) rebellion and violence; (2) hedonism (living for pleasure); (3) drug and alcohol abuse; (4) despondency, suicide or escapism; (5) satanism or occultism; (6) secular humanism and worldly commercialism. Let's look at each of those areas and see if Christian rock music is living up to the challenge of providing a healthy biblical alternative.

---

[1]Bill Huie, "Reflections, Distortions and Fragmentation," *Media Development* (Vol. XXIX), p. 10.

Angry Young Men

While mainstream rock music is perhaps most often indicted as a rabble-rouser, it errs by striking out against all the wrong things. Steve Taylor describes this sort of rebel perfectly in his song, "You've Been Bought": "This year's rock and roll messiah come to settle some old score/You can save the bad boy posturing, I've seen that sneer before/ You've been bought." "In the words of U2's Bono Hewson," explains Taylor, " 'You could actually write a rulebook on how to behave as a rock 'n' roll rebel.' This song is for all those who followed the rules."[2]

Many young people actually buy into that rebel cry. Jim Watke, a former mainstream deejay who now spins Christian hits, describes how music affected him when he was young. "These artists," he claims, "gave me the power inside to rebel against my parents. The power! I could hear them tell us to throw the books at our teachers. The devil, through the lyrics, gave me the power to stand up and live a rebellious lifestyle. It's like having the artist come in and take your kid's hand and say, 'Come on, let's tell your parents where it's at.' "

There is, however, a legitimate, biblical rebellion. It is against the "god of this world" and his authority. In the Scriptures, Isaiah and Amos are rebels in the best sense of the word. They exhibited anger and revulsion at the sinfulness and hypocrisy of their people. In the same way, Christian music, rock or middle-of-the-road, can appropriately present the virtuous side of rebellion. It can strike out against the wrongs it sees and fight for the right.

With their *When You're A Rebel* LP, the raucous-sounding Altar Boys say they're in the fight for the duration: "We oppose the prince of this world. His power and influence upon this earth has destroyed countless lives. We oppose the standards for living that contradict the Word of God. We oppose false religions that claim to enlighten and guide one's life and mind, yet are only lies that lead to eternal death. Being a rebel is a way of life. It's abiding and following our only hope in this world, Jesus Christ our Savior."

---

[2]Steve Taylor, *Media Update* (Vol. 5: Issue 2), p. 5.

A number of Christian rock groups are singing similarly challenging messages, but Petra has long stood out as one of the most vocal rebels against spiritual mediocrity. In "Stand Up" they shout out, "Stand up, take a stand for Jesus/Stand up, so the whole world sees us/ Showing the way to a world gone stray/ Shining our light with all of our might."

DeGarmo and Key also bring a confrontative note to much of their music. They say they want to "make Christians aware of an apathetic attitude that is sweeping the ranks and call them to action with such songs as 'Apathy Alert,' 'Casual Christian' and 'Activate.'" In "Activate," they ask the Lord to fill their hearts "with strength from above/ Lord, take away all of my apathy/ And give me the courage to love."

A rebel's call to the fight is the subject of many Servant tunes as well. In "Battlecry," they declare, "We need to stand and fight/ Sound the battle cry, it's time to choose your side." Likewise, the Swedish group Jerusalem sings in "Warrior," "We must join forces in battle/ And fight as one in the Son." Another well-established artist, Randy Stonehill, further provokes rebellion against this sinful, apathetic world when he sings, "He wants some angry young men/ Ones who can't be bought/ Ones who will not run from a fight."

The members of Philadelphia, a hard-rockin' band, who claim they appeal to "the marginal church kid who maybe has heard the gospel but is drifting into other things," also sing about rebellion. They aim, however, to reach the unrighteous kind of rebel in "Bobby's Song": "Oh, what can you say when he/ Turns love away and he's all on his own/ Outside he's so tough but inside/ It's a bluff and he feels so alone."

In terms of style, Cindy Richardson is on the other side of the spectrum, but she also sings about a sad, sinful rebel in "Doesn't He Know?": "Why is that child so angry/ Cursin' in the middle of the street/ . . . Doesn't he know about Jesus?/ . . . Who can set him free/From all his emptiness and misery."

As writer Jerry Solomon comments in *Shofar* magazine, "A sensitive chord is strummed when someone hears a song that aligns his feelings of frustration and anger."[3] However, if—

---

[3]Jerry Solomon, "Between Rock and a Hard Place," *Shofar* (Fall 1983), p. 11.

through music—that chord is strummed in such a way that youthful energy and idealism are channeled toward righteous rebellion, today's "angry young men"—and women—could change the world.

Hedonism: Love to Go

Hedonism, sexual permissiveness and, in some circles, even sexual abuse have been given a free hand in our society, largely due to attitudes promoted through the media—with rock music near the top of the list. Author/philosopher Edith Schaeffer cautions, "In the mishmash of today's standards of right and wrong, many children are being born into an atmosphere that is alien to the Ten Commandments, so alien that to simply state them would have no meaning at all."[4]

In no sector of life is this permissive atmosphere more alien to a Christian than in sexual standards. As early as 1977, *U.S. News & World Report* stated, "Unlike x-rated movies and books, this music is broadcast, performed in concerts and available on records to any listener, regardless of age."

Even some members of the record industry admit musicians abuse their power by writing trashy lyrics. George David Weiss, a representative of the Songwriters Guild, told a Senate committee hearing, "I deplore violent, sexually explicit themes. I don't underestimate the power of ideas, which are deadlier than bullets."[5]

Unfortunately, many adults do underestimate that power. In fact, most parents, according to Ethelynn Stuckey of the Parent Music Resource Center, "are unaware of the words their children are listening to, dancing to, doing homework to, falling asleep to."

Perhaps, as Jerry Williams, of the pop rock group Harvest theorizes, we have all grown complacent and slack: "If the real church in America were 100 million strong, we wouldn't see the

---

[4]Edith Shaeffer, "Lifelines," (Westchester, Ill.: Crossway Books, 1982), p. 143.
[5]*Broadcasting* (9/16/85), p. 39.

rampant degradation of our society so evident today."[6] Undoubtedly, we do need to wash ourselves clean continually from the residue of our society's sinfulness.

We should not, however, wash ourselves as Pilate did, supposedly clearing himself of all responsibility. We are all to blame for society's corruption and must do all we can to stop further decline. One way we can fight secular rock music's influence on the sexual mores of our youth is by promoting wholesome alternative lyrics.

When *Charisma* magazine asked Sandi Patti about the rock lyric controversy, she said, "Music is a very powerful force. It has a way of breaking down barriers. Sometimes when a speaker can't or a book can't, music can. But a lot of artists are taking that very powerful tool and putting negative, horrible lyrics to it, and those lyrics are getting into the hearts of the listeners and are shaping their values. . . . Why can't we take that same powerful force—music—put positive lyrics to it and begin shaping values that way?"[7]

A number of new Christian music artists are trying to do just that. Sometimes with a "heavy" message, sometimes in a simple way, they are introducing themes about the joy of falling in love in a righteous way, about the right kind of fun, about peer pressure and about the serious consequences of sexual immorality.

Billy Graham crusade soloist, as well as Christian rocker, Kenny Marks sings several songs about Johnny and Jeanie, two teenagers who learn too late the dangers of premarital sex. "Songs such as 'The Party's Over' bring a high school romance scene into play," Marks explains, "showing the consequences of confusing self-worth in a relationship. The lyrics, 'ain't it funny how infatuation fooled them into playing house,' clearly shows kids the effects of the unruly emotions in [the characters] Johnny and Jeanie. I sang this song at Great America near Chicago . . . and a hush fell over the audience. They just couldn't believe that this story was evolving right in front of them—and they knew that this song is about themselves."

---

[6]Susan Coker, "Harvest: Missionary in the Heartland," *Contemporary Christian* (11/85), p. 26.
[7]"Sandi Patti: In the Face of Change," *Charisma* (2/86), p. 43.

Pop vocalist Brent Lamb sings about the same kind of situation, viewed from a positive angle, in the tune, "Waiting Is Worth It" on his LP *Tug of War*: "In every life there comes a time/ When our hearts are tempted to stray/ . . .You must live by the Spirit/ With His strength you can wait/ Overcome the desires/ With patience and faith."

Waiting for God's timing is also the theme of a Stryper tune, "(Waiting For) a Love That's Real": "I love you, I want you,/ But that won't change the way I feel/ . . . She waits for a godly love/ Knowing that someday it will come from above."

Lyricist-turned-performer Michael W. Smith likewise treats the subject of sex realistically in "You Need a Savior": "Made a friend last night, or you thought you did/ Had a drink, had a talk, took a drive/ Shared the night, gave up a part of your soul/ Now she's gone and you're a little less alive." Reveals Smith, "I'm out to reach the 'peer pressure people' who have problems. It's tough being a teenager in the eighties—all the pressure for drugs and sex—I know from the mail I get and from seeing what kids are experiencing. It's tough and I'm out there to tell them there's an alternative—to say, 'Hey, there's a way out. You don't have to give in.' "

Triloję, a relatively new trio, provides several such songs on its debut album, including a Steve Camp/Rob Frazier-penned tune which warns of "Stolen Love": "Stolen Love, ah you had to taste it/ Stolen love, now it's caused you such pain/ Stolen love, now it's left you dry and wasted/ Now you know that love is not a game/ . . . It's a gift from God and we should treat it so."

Another young group, Twenty Twenty, tells about the danger of "Love to Go": "It's Friday night and the town's on fire/ And I'm a victim of my peers/ Can I break the code . . . repeated throughout the years/ . . . No more love to go."

The same frankness and realism are evident in Leslie Phillips' tune "I Won't Let it Come Between Us" from her *Dancing With Danger* LP: "You know wrong can sure look good sometimes/ And it's caught my eyes just like a jewel that shines." Similar, but more potent, is "Light of Love," in which she admits it's not always easy to wait for marriage: " . . . I want someone to hold me through the night/ I know that you are willing/ But . . . I can't walk away from what is right."

Says *Cornerstone* reviewer Jon Trott, "Honest without being cynical, always offering real answers to real problems, Leslie Phillips is an artistic and spiritual example to Christians young and old. We're never too old to learn the truth in love." Likewise, we're never too young or too old to learn the truth *about* love.

Jesus Can Make You Higher

From the booze-filled fifties to the cocaine-addicted eighties, mainstream rock music has often promised young people that drugs will give them power, peace and happiness. According to Dr. Paul King, director of adolescent services at Charter Lakeside Hospital in Memphis, Tenn., secular heavy metal music, with its emphasis on power and partying, is particularly suspect as a link to drug use. "Young people in our treatment program who are recovering from drug problems must give up heavy metal for at least a year, so that they are not overtaken again by feelings of resentment and hate, and the urge to 'party.'" According to King, teenagers can so closely identify with the messages in the music that "the lyrics become a philosophy of life, a religion."[8]

Christian rock music has not only the opportunity but the duty to present truth to teens looking for answers: not just that "dope" is for dopes, but that Jesus can transform life better than any chemical can.

In "Caught in an Unguarded Moment," the somewhat controversial Christian new-wave band, 77's, cautions about the effect drugs and alcohol can have on life—here and in the hereafter: "I saw a young girl fly over a Rocky Mountain brink/ She had had too much to drink/ She did not have time to think/ But it was far more than just her car/ That flew out of control/ She had gone over the edge/ Long before she'd lost her soul." Offers Mary Neely of Exit Records, the 77's label: "Our lyrics address the human condition, communicating as Jesus did with the masses—where they hurt, where they live, in language they can identify with."[9]

---

[8]Stephen Newman, "Lighten Up on 'Heavy Metal'," *U.S. Journal of Alcohol and Drug Dependences* (4/86).
[9]*Echoes* (Vol. 1), p. 9.

The Cruse, whose members formerly sang in the popular gospel group, the Cruse Family, also believe strongly that teens will identify with lyrics concerning chemical abuse. Leader Joe Cruse claims, "It's a tool in which we can reach out to those kids and say, first of all, we're musicians, and we don't take drugs, and we don't smoke dope, nor drink alcohol. We try to do that which morally God has dictated in His Word to do. We have the peace that he can give us—the strength to make it through the day—without any kind of extra help from chemicals."

Similarly, Steve Crumbacher, of the group bearing his name, reveals, "I write all my songs from a Christian perspective, from a Christian point of view. So while a secular artist may be telling a young kid to turn to drugs, or whatever, to solve their problems, I'd be telling them how the Lord could work out things."

David and the Giants sing about drugs from personal experience. Singer and songwriter David Huff, his twin brothers, Clayborn and Rayborn, and drummer Keith Thibodeaux (known for his role as little Ricky in the *I Love Lucy* show,) all formerly struggled with drug abuse. "I got to the end of the road," says Thibodeaux. "I was doing heroin, cocaine, LSD, Quaaludes, mescaline, you name it—and I drank quite a bit."[10]

Thibodeaux testifies that coming to a personal knowledge of Christ took away all his desires for drugs. Eventually he witnessed to the others, they were born again, and David and the Giants was formed. Now they sing that the Lord has things "under control": "Rainy days rainy nights/ Sometimes come our way/ Sometimes up sometimes down/ Your Word lets me know it's ok/ . . . No matter what the circumstance/ He's got it under control."

In the same vein is Rez Band's bluesy rendition of "Quite Enough": "Used to worship my doping/ Till my brains got up and fried/ I used to worship knowledge/ Thought it would set me free/ I found Jesus' love is quite enough for me."

Though Christian artists have an opportunity to help young people experience the genuine, eternal joy of the Lord instead of a phony, short-lived chemical high, they must be careful not to imply a walk with the Lord is just some sort of "supernatural

---

[10]*People*, (2/85), p. 99.

high." Lyrics that unrealistically claim, as Christian artist T-Bone Burnett says, that "they used to take a lot of dope, then they became a Christian, [and] now everything is rosy" are just as phony as secular lyrics that try to tell us drugs are utopian. Claims Burnett, "I've found that being a Christian makes life 100,000 times more difficult than just being a sort of standard, run-of-the-mill hedonist."[11]

On the other hand, truly joyful music, reminding us of all the Lord has done for us, can lift a person's spirits, and there are times when each of us could use an antidote to depression or hopelessness. One such joy-filled, bright reminder is Angie Lewis's "Heartdance": "TV's telling me all the bad news/ Sayin' it's an offer that I can't refuse/ . . . Livin' in the promise of a day/ When love will pick me up and carry me away/ Hey I can hear those echoes of the Good News/ And I believe the promise so I just can't lose/ When I think of all I've been given/ And all that waits for me/ . . . It's makin' my heart dance."

Another hope-filled tune comes from a Christian pop group called Bash -n- the Code. They encourage their listeners to "Go ahead and sing like crazy/ Go ahead and dance like mad/ Shout out your praise to Jesus/ Don't hold your voices back." While such lyrics might initially shock those of us with more conservative tastes, we must remember that many Scripture references encourage God's people to do the same thing—to "shout for joy"—and several more suggest dancing for joy. The Lord, it seems, must be pleased with both.

And while the decibel level of some of this new Christian music isn't necessarily what we personally prefer, we remind ourselves that John's Revelation describes worship in heaven as the singing of "a new song," by huge multitudes, and shouting "in a loud voice" by millions of angels and every living creature in the universe—all in praise to God. Such a description is reminiscent of the cacophony of a Christian rock concert!

Furthermore, when the Pharisees demanded Jesus subdue the shouting, rejoicing crowds who followed him, he replied, "I tell you, if these should hold their peace, the stones would im-

---

[11]*Wittenburg Door* (Issue 80), p. 24.

mediately cry out" (Luke 19:37–41). The Pharisees tried to stifle the crowd's festive spirit because of their own stuffy, cultural biases. In the spirit of Jesus, however, we can and should overcome cultural preferences tempting us to silence youthful, exuberant praise. Songs such as these can give teenagers hope and joy, add backbone to their resolve to say "no" to peer pressure and plug into their God-given energy and zest for life.

Don't Say Suicide

In Proverbs we read, "What you say can preserve life or destroy it . . ." (Prov. 18:21, GNB). The passage then says each of us will be held accountable for what we say—a frightening thought given the content of many of today's top secular hits. Says Christian record producer Mary Neely, "Over the last five years or so, the new sounds, punk and new wave, have been full of despair, nihilistic even. Especially the groups from England."[12]

Here is an opportunity for lyricists and artists to shine God's truth on the world's darkness. Unfortunately, as the late Francis Schaeffer said, many traditional songwriters "have not even thought of the problem, much less the answer."[13]

Responding to the frequency of teenage suicides in the news, a number of Christian rock songwriters have recently risen to the challenge to provide sensitive lyrics, realism, life and hope for their troubled young listeners.

Mike States, a lyricist, producer and president of an independent Christian record label, points out, "If nothing else, we must convey the fact that life is worth living and life does have purpose. The Police may be technically clever and melodious, but can find and share no meaning or hope. I pity poor rich man Sting, gaining the whole world . . ."[14]

Artists such as Sting, espousing a "what's the use?" philosophy—whether through arrogance or ignorance—may implant in impressionable young minds permission to commit suicide. In opposition, Second Chapter of Acts' Anne Herring insists, "I

---

[12]*Echoes*, Ibid., p. 8.
[13]"The Battle for Our Culture," *New Wine* (2/82), p. 9.
[14]Mike States, "The States Report," *New Christian Media* (Vol. 3, #4).

think that people . . . have a responsibility to recognize that their words hold the power of life or death. . . . I want whatever I say to have the power of life."[15]

Rocco Marshall talks about the power of words in Vision's "Don't Say It's Over": "I heard you talking and that talk could take you under/ Foolish words, desperate rage can steal your life away/ I know your future seems so dark and endless/ Don't let your fears put you in the grave. . . . Don't say it's over." Cautions Marshall, "Subliminally, the devil feeds these kids all kinds of junk. And what he's doing there is preaching a lie through incredibly good advertising." Marshall insists his music is aimed at fighting those lies, and supplying teenagers with life-giving truth.

Angie Lewis's hit, "Silent Weeper," is another good example of this offence against suicide: "Don't give up on love, there's no need to fear," she proclaims to the silent yet sorrow-filled. "Jesus still loves you. He can heal your heart, for He too has scars, and He knows how sorrow feels."

Lewis explains, "I've seen people are hurting. We need more healing songs. That's what 'Weeper' is and what I've tried to stress with this song is that we have to accept this healing and live there in it. It's always there for us, but we have to turn and accept it."

Accomplished Christian female vocalist, Teri DeSario—who formerly sang with the secular group, K.C. and the Sunshine Band—also offers her listeners hope and self-worth in the bittersweet tune, "Voices in the Wind," in which she sings of a child abuse victim who carries into adulthood suicidal feelings of guilt and shame. However, the "voices in the wind," which are actually quotes from Scripture as well as from great mystics such as Teresa of Avila, Meister Eckhart and Julian of Norwich, remind her that "life is to be lived," that she is made in the image of God, and that God sees her as lovable and beautiful and good.

Kathy Troccoli, who also sang for the secular market before accepting Christ, relates, "Kids nowadays—especially with the teen suicide—suffer from purposelessness. They've got everything, but they don't have purpose. Well, Jesus gives you purpose. I tell kids if I wasn't singing, I'd still have purpose because

---

Jesus lives inside me, and I try to bring that encouragement and message to young people."

Troccoli's tune, "Hearts of Fire," persuades young people not to turn cold or give in to desperation, but to "Stand by the power living in us/ He's given us hearts of fire."

"Weight of the World," a Rob Frazier tune, and "Don't Say Suicide," sung by Rick Cua, offer more of the same. Frazier asks, "Do you feel like a lonely soul in the city tonight?/ Struggling to survive but it's a losing fight/ Hurting and crying just look at you/ You're slowly dying/ But Jesus can take your heavy load." Likewise, Cua declares, "Don't say suicide/ It's your move consider it well/ . . .The choice is life or the lie that comes from hell."

A newer group, Terms of Peace, has taken its name seriously, offering songs such as "I Think I Know": "I think I know how you feel/ You've lost the one you thought cared/ I know it hurts— it hurts me too/ . . .Why don't we take off all our masks/ And see where we could go from there."

Ministering as an integral part of a community of reconciliation, Servant also sings of hope: "Yesterday the ashes/ Today the hope, the dream restored/ Through life and death, passion and pain/ His timeless love remains the same." Likewise, the story teller-singer Carman reminds his young fans that Jesus is real: "Fear not my child/ I'm with you always/ I feel every pain/ And every tear I see/ . . . I know how to care for what belongs to me."

Undercover's O-Joe Taylor maintains that hopelessness and suicide are issues the church needs to deal with simply because they exist. "We can't just 'devil' them away," he insists. Taylor sings of suicide in the song, "In My Darkest Hour": "Hanging by a thread and out of control/ Could things be worse if I were dead? There's people here, but I'm so alone . . . In my darkest hour, I need You there."

Kenny Metcalf is the keyboardist for Stryper, the Christian heavy-metal band whose unorthodox appearance and music have unsettled many believers with more conservative tastes. Metcalf is also the "friend" Stryper's members credit with persuading them to give their lives to the Lord. Though the group's methods may be debatable, Metcalf's point is well-taken—he exhorts young people, "Listen to music that has a good message.

Listen to something that edifies you and builds you up, instead of tearing you down. . . . I don't put on songs of suicide. . . . I want to listen to something that's going to encourage me and help me through the day—a positive message." With at least ten percent of America's high school students toying with thoughts of suicide at this moment, Metcalf's observations take on added importance.

Unmasking the Deceiver

After one of Leon Russell's concerts, his manager remarked, "Leon knows he can awake spiritual power in his audience." The secular artist, according to his manager, "knows he has power and enjoys feeling it."[16] Likewise, Gordon Gano, professing Christian as well as lead singer of unconventional group, Violent Femmes, maintains, "Music by its very nature is very spiritual. Any kind of music can be interpreted in a spiritual way. There's something so magical about."[17]

With music able to wield such tremendous power over the spiritual life of the listener, lyrics—especially those in heavy metal—that deal particularly with the spiritual realm possess added clout. In a *Today Show* interview on satanism and the occult, psychiatrist Alfred Coutelly referred to Richard Ramirez, the so-called Night Stalker. Coutelly said, "He heard this band—the AC/DC band—playing the song, 'The Night Prowler,' and the lyrics, the words of that song, echo accurately what he actually carried out. So in a certain sense, he was identifying with that particular song and the contents of it in his actions."

Likewise, Dr. Paul King, an expert in dealing with teenage substance abuse, told a Senate subcommittee hearing in Washington, D.C.: "Every teenager who listens to heavy metal certainly does not become a killer. But young people who are seeking power over others through the identification with the power of evil find a close identification in heavy metal."

King revealed that drawings by his adolescent patients

---

[16]LaMar Boschman, *The Rebirth of Music* (Little Rock, Ark.: Manasseh Books, 1980), p. 21, as quoted from *Empire.*
[17]*St. Paul Pioneer Press and Dispatch* (6/13/85), p. 5D.

showed signs of that identification, including pentagrams, up-side-down crosses and the numbers 666—the biblical "mark of the Beast."[18]

When asked why there has been such an overtly demonic element in rock music, Kerry Livgren, who leads the Christian group A.D., responded: "Because it's such a powerful communication medium. The medium itself is so able to communicate a concept, we have to expect that it will be an area where Satan is going to concentrate his efforts. . . . I don't think there's a real insidious plot in [the artists' minds] to corrupt kids. . . . I think that they are being used, very definitely. And I think they are as sad as the kids who listen to it."[19]

The situation is a dark one, but very few Christian musicians are supplying a positive substitute. One group reaching out to the teenager fascinated by the dark side is Stryper. While this and other Christian hard rock groups often raise Christian parents' eyebrows, Pat Boone, popular entertainer and host of a Christian music video show, argues bands such as Stryper "are speaking the kids' language, but they are getting a different message than they are hearing from W.A.S.P. . . . or Mötley Crüe, or all these other groups that sing about sadomasochism and bestiality and drugs and suicide and actual Satanism. . . . Kids understand that message."

Robert Sweet of Stryper adds, "God has called us to be a light in a dark place—and rock and roll is a dark place—but the light can shine brighter in a dark place." On their *Yellow and Black Attack* LP, Stryper sings, "So many bands give the devil all the glory/ It's hard to understand, we want to change the story." Michael Sweet says they're serious about changing that story. "God is going to raise up a standard today. 'When the enemy comes in like a flood, the Lord raises up a standard.' Well, in rock and roll, a new standard is being raised up and we're happy about it."

Equally active in fighting satanic influence through lyrics is Lenny LeBlanc, whose tune, "Someday," asks, "Do you pick up

---

[18]Stephen Newman, "Lighten Up on 'Heavy Metal'," *U.S. Journal of Alcohol and Drug Dependence* (4/86).

[19]Foster Braun, "Kerry Livgren, Inside Rock," *Windstorm* (Vol. 1: No. 3), p. 40.

the morning paper/ Just to read your horoscope/Are you looking at the moon and the stars/ Just so you can hope/ It's all just a lie from the devil/ No matter what they tell ya."

A number of other artists are now beginning to warn against the occult and friendship with the devil—Englishman Cliff Richard's "Devil Woman"; Bob Dylan's "Gotta Serve Somebody"; Steve Taylor's "Drive, He Said"; Rob Frazier's "666"; Petra's "Pied Piper"; A.D.'s "Mask of the Deceiver"; and DeGarmo and Key's "Six, Six, Six." There is even a non-music Christian comedy album, Eternal Vision's *Special Deliverance*, the first in a satirical series intended to knock Satan's sock's off.

Perhaps the best way to combat secular rock's satanic bent, though, is a counter-offensive of true worship music. Sadly enough, most Christian young people today possess a very limited, inaccurate picture of who God is and why we should praise Him.

"Isn't it funny that demons know more about the nature of God than most church kids?" youth evangelist Winkie Pratney asks, referring to the two demoniacs in Matthew's gospel who addressed Jesus as the "Son of God." Unfortunately, Pratney's right. However with today's emphasis on music, contemporary Christian tunes can help our young people come to know the Lord better. Of course, it must not only meet kids "where they're at," but also take them to a higher place.

By worship music we are not talking only about traditional church hymns. Though traditional church hymns are edifying and play an important part in worship, there are also many excellent worship tunes within Christian rock music. Not only do these tunes appeal to the youthful ear, they can heighten appreciation of God just as skillfully as traditional music.

At concerts and festivals across the country, we've watched young people come to know and worship the Lord, through both the music and the spoken messages. Though we experienced an initial bout with "culture shock," we were delighted to see young people—some wearing bandanas and carefully torn jeans, or leather jackets and orange hair—praising God to music filled with guitar licks and drum solos!

Glenn Kaiser, who blasts the air with Rez Band's hard-rock

hallelujahs, often reminds his audiences about their need for more than "feel good" music: "You see, folks, when we gather together, it's not just to rock and roll, but it's to worship and adore the Lord. So as we share our little bit here, we want to start it off with every eye closed and head bowed.

"Let's sing a chorus of 'Oh, Come Let Us Adore Him,' because I want to adore the Lord this afternoon. As you applaud Rez Band and all the folks that are going to sing, don't just applaud them because you like what they are doing, but because you see Jesus in them and you want Him lifted up."

"There's something really powerful about concentrating on what God Almighty has done," claims Amy Grant[20], and Christian rock music offers a wide variety of ways to do just that— from Grant's lullaby-like "El-Shaddai" to Rez Band's power-packed "I'm So In Love With You"; from Larnelle Harris's soulful "Amen," to Randy Stonehill's unique "Love Beyond Reason"; from the hot harmonies of Petra's "Praise Ye the Lord," to the velvet-soft vocals of Glad's "Champion of Love."

Shallow Water

Innocent-sounding, wayward messages, tied up in pretty, tuneful packages are secular rock's bread and butter. The performers even admit to it, calling the worst examples "bubble gum" music. In hot pursuit of the almighty dollar, rock music artists often offer this poisonous fluff as if it were golden nuggets of pure truth.

Unfortunately, Christian music creators, past and present, have sometimes been just as shallow and commercial in their approach to writing and producing music, portraying God as some sort of cosmic Wizard of Oz and the Christian way of life as a skip down a yellow brick road. Christian artists/producers/ writers Tom Howard and Bill Batstone, in a slightly sardonic take-off on Philippians 4:8, admit entertainers are often tempted to think on "whatsoever is cute/ Whatsoever is elating/ Whatsoever favors you with heightened media ratings."

---

[20] "My Favorite Lyrics Are . . ." *Christian Life* (2/84), p. 64.

The challenge is to go beyond cute and get at the heart of God. As talented songwriter Greg Nelson maintains, "In the secular market, you only have to be a good craftsman. You don't necessarily have to have anything good to say. But in the religious market, you have to be a great craftsman and have spiritual depth, and that's really hard. We don't have a lot of great writers."

Dave Edwards, leader of a band bearing his name, agrees there is a tendency to turn lyrics into nothing more than bubble gum Bible verse: "Some people seem able to follow the precedents of praise in the Bible, but not things like Job, the Song of Solomon, Ecclesiastes, and Lamentations. . . . My goal is to be as close with God as possible and do what he wants me to do. . . . The important thing is that I am more anxious to be obedient than I am anxious to be bought in the music industry."[21]

Providing a musical product that has real value and yet is commercially viable often proves difficult work. However, Christian artists owe their fans, and especially the Lord, their very best. They command, after all, the attention of millions of people, and have a platform on which to preach timeless truths.

Just as artists need to guard against giving cheap answers and search for real meaning and truth, we listeners must demand the very best lyrics from artists, even in music created primarily for entertainment. Unfortunately, we take little time to appreciate quality things and search out quality answers. As the late statesman Adlai Stevenson once said, "As scarce as truth is, the supply seems greater than the demand."

We blindly swallow faulty philosophies and are willingly sucked in by shallow commercialism. The Christian rock band Prodigal says we often discount time-honored values and ideas, accepting the "Next Best Thing": "In a world of too many answers/ Why do questions seem so large/ Take your pick; Got your choice of cancers free of charge/ . . . I keep waiting for Elvis/ I keep wondering 'bout Dylan/ I keep crying for the Beatles/ Waiting for the next best thing."

---

[21]Glenn Kaiser, "Interview, Dave Edwards," *Cornerstone* (Vol. 13: Issue 71), p. 42.

We don't want to imply that every catchy, commercially successful song is a cheap product, however. A "hook" or memorable refrain in a song can do just that—it can be a memory aide, actually adding more power to lyrics. Furthermore, commercial success does not—by itself—indicate shallow lyrics any more than Billy Graham's success as an evangelist indicates he preaches a cheap gospel.

What we are discussing, however, is the truthfulness of the message presented. Our music can offer a simple truth ("Jesus loves me this I know,/ For the Bible tells me so") or a profound truth, but it must be truth or it's of no deep, lasting value. Instead, it's as the lyrically honest group Servant sings, "Shallow Water." It has no depth, no value.

Calvin Miller wrote about this shallowness in his classic allegory, *The Singer*. In the story, the character representing Jesus asks the World Hater (representing the devil), "How did you manage to make them cherish all this nothingness?"

The World Hater answers, "I simply make them feel embarrassed to admit that they are incomplete. . . . I sell a cheaper product."[22]

In music lyrics, as in every area of our lives, we must be sure we never settle for a cheaper product. Rather than accept cheap, throw-away words in music, let's keep in mind what the Christian new-wave group, Edin-Adahl, sings: that we can be "accepted and resurrected by your words/ . . . infiltrated and well instructed by your words." As Helen Keller suggested, let's never be satisfied with less than soul-awakening, freedom-giving, power-filled lyrics.

---

[22]Calvin Miller, "The Singer" (Downers Grove, Ill.: InterVarsity Press, 1977), p. 81.

Chapter Seven

Lifestyles

While riding the crest of popularity, a superstar's influence seems awesome. Whether the image is illusion or not, the power seems quite real.

—*Author Steve Lawhead*

The trash-flash superstar idol, Madonna, has been constantly surrounded by scores of pre-teen, lace- and pearl-draped fans who mimic their idol right down to the moles on the upper lip. Likewise, when porno popstar Prince adopted purple and paisley, both color and print became instant high fashion.

If young fans were simply to copy rock clothing styles there would be less need for concern (although often even the clothing is morally objectionable). However, mainstream rock and roll has proven to affect more than mere clothing trends. Whether a rock star exhibits admirable qualities or revels in a totally wasted lifestyle, he has a platform from which he influences the lives and morals of millions of young people. Given the hyped, highly visible lifestyle of many secular rock superstars, and our society's love affair with celebrity, artists possess awesome powers of influence.

"Idol worship in America," insists author and rock music critic Steve Lawhead, "has always taken a novel approach. Our idols of stage and screen are lifted to fantastic heights on waves of popular appeal. . . . While riding the crest of popularity, a super star's influence seems awesome. Whether the image is illusion or not, the power seems quite real."[1]

---

[1]Steve Lawhead, *Rock Reconsidered* (Downers Grove, Ill.: InterVarsity Press, 1981), p. 39.

Through a scientifically documented process known as "modeling," individuals have been shown to exhibit previously prohibited behavior merely by observing the actions of another. In the same way, fans emulate their favorite rock stars, even when the artists' influence is unintentional.

Of course, young people who enjoy Christian music may mimic the lifestyles of their favorite artists too. Once again, fashions are the most obvious, but some young fans also walk like, talk like, and look like their Christian music heroes. When Amy Grant bounces onstage in her baggy leopard-print jacket, dozens of Grant groupies in the audience display similarly spotted attire, and Stryper's "yellow and black attack" concerts host swarms of bumble-bee-decked teens. We will discuss this matter of visuals in a later chapter. At this point we are focusing on behaviors.

Thousands of young fans are also swayed when a highly visible Christian star gives testimony of how the Lord is working in his life. That is one of the most powerful aspects of Christian contemporary music—its power to change lives for the good. The opposite, of course, is also true. Teens are adversely affected when they emulate a popular Christian artist who, though claiming commitment to Christ, presents a bad example when he drinks or smokes in public, uses improper or indiscreet language or exhibits immoral behavior.

In a real sense, performers are teachers. As such, they bear responsibility for what they teach—not only with their words and music, but also with their lives. On the whole, they seem to take this burden seriously, leading a very different lifestyle from their secular contemporaries. However, music artists are human, and the music business is not without its pitfalls and pressures. It follows then, that some artists, no matter what their musical style, have or will make mistakes. Occasionally, we hear reports of drug abuse, sexual sin, faltering marriages and even crime. And perhaps there will always be those prone to greed, self-centeredness or shallowness.

Our purpose in this book is not to condemn our brothers and sisters. We realize Christian entertainers are as human and as prone to error as any of us. Referring to the many temptations faced by young people like herself, actress-singer Lisa Welchel assures, "These things are not more difficult because I'm in show business. They're difficult because I'm human."[2]

Therefore, rather than critique Christian entertainers' private lives, our aim is to discuss how their public images and lifestyles affect us all: What is it actually like to be a Christian rock artist—do they truly enjoy a glamorous lifestyle? How should we react to news about "back-slidden" Christian entertainers? Should we believe everything we read about rock stars' lives? Are Christians sometimes too judgmental of Christian rock stars' private lives? How are we to judge Christian contemporary music artists' lifestyles? What is the artist's responsibility to young people?

What is it actually like to be a Christian rock artist—do they truly enjoy a glamorous lifestyle?

The rock 'n' roll lifestyle—whether mainstream or Christian—isn't all we envision it to be. Young people and parents alike often picture entertainers' lives as being one glamorous event after another—from party to press conference to performance and back to party.

The artists tell a different story, however—especially Christian artists who often sacrifice much to pursue a ministry-career. Terry Taylor of the Christian group, Daniel Amos Band, explains, "At one time I was very idealistic about going out on the road. I had very romantic notions about doing this sort of thing and playing music and having people accept my music and pat me on the back and say, 'You're great.' But after you've been doing it for so many years, it's work. It's not just a kick. . . . It's a challenge and it's hard, and a lot of times absolutely no fun at all. I think that's the way God keeps us from having ego trips."

Likewise, veteran Christian contemporary music groups such as Rez Band, Dallas Holm and Praise, Petra, and Servant tell tales of equipment breakdowns, late-night traveling in old, cramped station wagons and vans, disappointing turnouts and frustrating financial problems—situations we never imagine when we watch them onstage with the flashy lights and entertaining sounds.

---

[2]*Contemporary Christian* (4/83), p. 14.

"What they don't see," maintains Holm, "is the sometimes all-night drive you have to make to the next city, the living out of a suitcase. . . . There are a lot of sacrifices to be made and it's physically demanding—you keep late hours, set up and tear down. It's also emotionally and psychologically demanding, especially in the ministry work, where you are counseling with people and problems. Every night, you're dealing with young people and adults with problems—everything from suicide to drugs to unwanted pregnancy to sexuality. It's all there and they're looking to you for some kind of help and you give out emotionally and you give out spiritually."

Somewhat newer on the scene is Bulgarian-born Christian artist Georgian Banov, but he agrees both secular and Christian music fields are tough. "The secular music business is a terrible place to be because of the lifestyle, the corruption, and all that. But even for Christians the touring, doing shows night after night, is a drag of a life. I would not recommend it to anyone except those who have a calling from the Lord to do it as a ministry for God. The hard part is spiritual. We are attacking the devil's territory and the devil gets upset. We get real spiritual attacks. Offstage, coming off a tour, we are exhausted."

Not only is the touring life not all one would expect, but the rock star's home life is seldom like the glittering image we see in front of the spotlights. Rez Band's Wendi Kaiser appears onstage in multi-colored, multi-layered costumes, with hair and eye makeup just as rainbow-like.

However, she says her daily life at Jesus People USA, a community in uptown Chicago, is unadorned and simple: "Everyone I live with marvels at the transformation that takes place on the weekends. You know, 'Here she is the nice housewife, the pastor's wife, momma to five, who counsels the kids, takes in the kids, and then on the weekends she turns into the rock and roll momma!' And it is so hilarious, such an about-face, but I do it only because I love Jesus and I remember what it was like to be a teenager."

Though there are exceptions, most Christian artists, when at home, also live a simple life, much like the average person. They spend time with their families, serve in various capacities with their fellowships—from pastor to choir member to custodian. Though there are some commercially successful artists, many drive vintage cars and hold down second jobs to keep their music ministries going. At home they trade the glittery stage clothes for work clothes, and the applause for children's laughter. After cooking meals, changing diapers, shopping for groceries and doing household chores, they squeeze in time to rehearse for their next gig or record.

How should we react to news about "backslidden" Christian entertainers?

Our culture is celebrity-happy and often we put those in the arts on pedestals. While the view from atop a pedestal may be heady, being constantly in the public eye also has its dangers. Don Basham, former editor of *New Wine* magazine, writes, "It is a cunning tactic for discord that Satan uses when he tricks us into putting people on pedestals, for the moment they fall off we begin to resent and criticize them. . . . The truth is, people almost always fall short of our expectations. Many times, however, the problem is not so much poor performance on their part as unreasonable expectations on ours."[3]

Dallas Holm brings up another drawback to pedestal status: "One of the most frustrating aspects of my ministry, my career, is that simply because of what I do—not who I am, but what I do, because I make records, I sit in front of a television camera, or stand on a stage with a bunch of lights and a lot of people— that in the eyes of people, it makes me separate, different, unique or special. And I think it's unfortunate we elevate artistic people to some level they don't deserve. Music is not any more wonderful than what anyone else can do and there are not categories of talents—these are really good ones, these are bad ones."

If we could forget the celebrity stigma and the hype, and learn to accept artistic people as Holm suggests, simply people blessed with one kind of gift while others are blessed with different gifts, we would be less tempted to mimic them even when they are in error. We would also be less likely to unlovingly attack or desert them when they show their fallibility.

When Bob Dylan sought Christianity for the answers to the

---

[3]Don Basham, "For Statues Only," *New Wine* (2/86), p. 36.

musical questions he'd been asking all his life, many pounced on him, eager to bring his aura of celebrity into the Christian camp. We proclaimed "Dylan—Saved!" and—before he could even discover what he was saved from—he again proclaimed "Dylan—Lost!"

Evangelist George Verwer asks, "Why do so many backslide if they are famous and they get saved? Because they are right in our eyes until they make their first big mistake—they get about 15 fundamentalist arrows in their backs! . . . It's judging people categorically, irrevocably, with no chance for explanations—that's what's so sad." It is sad.

Dylan has now declared his spiritual life off-limits, publicly speaking, and we may never know why (or even if) he has fallen away. We have to admit, we too, are perplexed by this man. However, if Dylan is once again lost, we must bear not just the loss, but also some of the blame, for rather than allowing him to proceed slowly as a pilgrim with the rest of us on the road of faith, we made him a pedestal person—demanding he instantly possess the wisdom of Solomon.

B. J. Thomas's career reveals a similar story. In 1976, following years of heavy drug addiction, Thomas announced he had given his life to the Lord and was free of drugs. Christians flocked to see their newest born-again star and to make his records bestsellers. Unfortunately, however, Thomas's Christian music career and his witness have been darkened by a sometimes zigzag lifestyle as well as a reputation for arrogance and rudeness.

As the editors of the *Wittenburg Door* pointed out, following a shocking yet revealing interview of Thomas, "We are very disappointed in B. J. Thomas but, unfortunately, we Christians bear some of the responsibility for what he's become. We were so anxious to use him when he was publicly expressing his new-found faith that we forgot to act responsibly ourselves. We were so anxious to sign him up for our TV specials, our record companies, our concerts, that we forgot about him. We used him. We sucked out of him every ounce of benefit we could get for our own personal gain."[4]

---

[4]"Loser of the Month: B.J. and the D.J.," *Wittenburg Door* (8–9/84), p. 23.

Amy Grant has been the focus of a similar love-hate struggle. Since she signed her first recording contract at the tender age of 15, she has earned three Grammys, numerous Dove Awards, sold out Radio City Music Hall, and has sold more records than any other contemporary Christian music artist. However, she also literally has had to grow up both physically and spiritually in the public eye. With characteristic youthful impetuousness, she has made mistakes and raised more than a few eyebrows over the last few years.

However, Melinda Scruggs, Grant's publicist, reveals, "Amy freely admits to not being 'perfect,' and [she] requests your prayers as she grows in Christ. Many of her mistakes have been made painfully public. She has asked for and received forgiveness from the people with whom she is accountable."

In that statement we find the difference between the worldly attitude of today's secular rock star, versus the attitude Christian artists must develop in order to survive the celebrity limelight: humility.

In the Bible, another musician-artist, King David, exemplified that same attitude. As king, the most powerful "celebrity" of his day, David stole another man's wife and had the man killed. However, David must have understood the tremendous influence he had over others who looked up to him and patterned their lives after his, because once his sin was exposed, he quickly and humbly repented. Though not a perfect man, David's heart attitude pleased God immensely.

David was also willing to be candid with his music. He sang not only about the joys of being God's beloved, but he often confessed his faults (cf. Ps. 32:5; 38; 51), and wrote truthfully of the pain it caused (Ps. 32:3–4; 77:1–10). Real spiritual life can spring from truthful, open confession, and David's fearless honesty—in his life as well as his music—breathed life into both.

As David, Christian artists, whatever their musical style, must all strive to be honest, climbing off the celebrity pedestal to acknowledge their imperfections, and if necessary, to ask forgiveness both of God and of others to whom they are accountable. In some situations, that may mean a public confession. Steve Griffith, of the Christian pop group Vector, believes many Christian entertainers want to "hide the fact that they're human. I think that once you do that, the very people you're trying to talk to won't be able to relate to you because they've picked up on a kind of superior attitude from you. . . . The farthest thing from my mind is to develop an elitist attitude—'us' and 'them.' I'm just doing the best I can at what I do. And I'd just like to help whomever I can along the way."[5]

O-Joe Taylor of Undercover also insists it's important they not keep their faults under wraps: "We were not all that neat and pretty and clean when we became Christians," he tells his fans. "We have a lot of problems, and God deals with us. It's a walk with God, a slow process in pursuit of holiness, but God has helped us and . . . he will help you too." With this kind of attitude, Christian rock groups can take the lessons learned from their failings and turn them into life-giving tunes.

But if someone fails we must treat him as any brother in Christ. We can pray for him, confront him (by writing a letter), and avoid spreading gossip—which may not be true. Our task is to restore and build him up, not to destroy his reputation.

Should we believe everything we read about rock stars' lives?

Just as we must be discerning listeners, we must also become discriminating readers. We need to bear in mind that the secular press—and to some extent even the Christian press—does not know what to do with a Christian celebrity. According to *Public Opinion* magazine, only 8 percent of the media elite in the U.S. attend a church or synagogue regularly and 86 percent seldom or never go to services. When asked their religious affiliation, the magazine says, half of U.S. media people responded "none."[6] Therefore it's not surprising the secular press knows little concerning Christian terminology and values, or that it uses worldly terms which translate poorly in the Christian market.

When contemporary-looking and sounding Christian performers such as Amy Grant, Stryper, Sheila Walsh or Steve Taylor begin to get noticed, the secular media don't know how to classify them. Likewise, the media's warped sense of what con-

[5]Jon Trott, "Vector," *Cornerstone* (Vol. 14: Issue 76), p. 37.
[6]*Public Opinion* (10–11/1981).

stitutes Christianity also muddles the picture. Consequently, the press describes Christian singer Sheila Walsh as "sexy," while labeling porn queen Madonna "born again"; they tag Christian performer Leslie Phillips the "Cyndi Lauper of Christian rock" and dub Prince the "Prince of Peace." When Amy Grant is touted "the Madonna of Christian rock" by one magazine article writer, several other publications pick it up. Eventually the phrase appears in the religious press, where it offends many Christian readers. Rather than criticize the writer, however, readers often blame the singer.

Certainly, few take seriously reports that Madonna and Prince are true believers, but many are puzzled and dismayed when Christian artists are described by the media in shocking terms. To be fair, we must carefully weed out the fuzzy thinking of the secular press. As George Barna, co-author of "Vital Signs: Emerging Social Trends and the Future of American Christianity," cautions: "We have reached the point where we can no longer allow the media to define what Christian means, how Christianity is or should be exemplified in our words and actions, or which individuals are placed on the media pedestal as examples of true believers. Without becoming judgmental of others, and with a spirit of love, we need to reclaim—and restore—a holy heritage that a misguided media are steadily destroying."[7]

As fans of Christian music, then, we need to separate the facts from the media's misguided hype. Furthermore, we need to be wary of less-than-innocent misunderstandings. Many in the secular press actually enjoy stirring up controversy surrounding Christians, pouncing on vicious rumors and searching out the most remote embarrassing details of Christian celebrities' lives.

As writer Terry Mattingly notes, "There is only one type of religion story editors love—a scandal."[8] After all, faults—especially a Christian's faults—make better stories than do virtues. Consequently, a *Rolling Stone* interviewer followed Amy Grant around for days, catching every off-hand remark and private conversation, then published a story focusing on several indis-

---

[7]George Barna, "The American Media Myth," *Spirit* (9–10/85), p. 13.

[8]Terry Mattingly, The Quill (January 1983), as quoted in *Book Burning*, by Cal Thomas (Westchester Ill.: Crossway Books, 1983), p. 112.

creet remarks rather than drawing from the hours of polite conversation. Furthermore, many statements—insist both Grant's publicist and her tour director—were taken out of context or incorrectly quoted.

Explains Melinda Scruggs, "The nature of an interview, whether it is in print or via the electronic media, is that the audience only gets a tiny slice of a conversation or thought. Many times the editing process can completely change the intent of a person's response."

The result can be very embarrassing and frustrating for an artist such as Grant, who attempts to be frank and uninhibited in her interviews and often suffers for it at the hand of an editor. "Please bear this in mind before passing judgment on what you perceive that Amy believes," Scruggs says. "The intent of her heart is to show the world Jesus' love. Her way may be different than your way [but] what she is doing is bearing fruit. . . ."

Handling the media can be extremely difficult and very tiring. In fact, we have often had our own words taken out of context, misunderstood or deliberately misquoted. We, too, have suffered the embarrassment of blurting out a hasty or inappropriate remark only to have it be the only quote used from a grueling hour-long interview. (Of course we are not excusing any inappropriate remark, just admitting our own humanness.)

It is also true, however, that if Grant (or any artist) is grooming to be a major crossover entertainer—appealing to the non-Christian as well as the Christian—she must develop the wisdom and finesse necessary to deal with a demanding media. She must overcome childish impetuousness, and strive toward thoughtful consideration of every remark, every action.

While we don't want to seem harsh, we believe Grant and other crossover artists owe it to their fans to remember Jesus' warning to His disciples: "I send you out as sheep in the midst of wolves; so be wise as serpents and innocent as doves" (Matt. 10:16, RSV). Christian contemporary musicians are quite literally sheep among wolves, and they need to work very hard maintaining their Christian witness in an ever-darkening environment.

Are Christians sometimes too judgmental of Christian rock stars' private lives?

Unfortunately, Christian artists are sometimes among wolves even in their own camp. Recently, we received a letter in our office from a well-meaning parent who demanded to know why we supported a certain artist who had behaved "scandalously." The letter then cited three examples, not one of which proved to be accurate, supposedly quoted from a source which was also in error. This wasn't the first time we had heard a potentially damaging, yet untrue story spread by well-meaning Christians.

Rumor-mongering of this sort not only harms the artist, it also presents a bad witness to non-Christians because it destroys the only way some non-believers will learn about Christianity— by how we love one another. When we tongue-wag about the private lives of Christian artists, it is sinful gossiping, no different than talking over the back fence about a next-door neighbor. Artists' private lives are simply nothing we should be discussing. Nonetheless, we often insist on knowing every detail of an artist's personal life.

Philip Bailey, who performs with the secular group Earth, Wind and Fire, as well as records Christian music, complains about prying individuals: "You just say, 'I'm a Christian, and I did a gospel album,' and then the people want to know what color underwear you wear, do you put your socks on right foot or left foot first, do you ask God about what kind of gas to use in your car? You wouldn't believe the letters that you get from people."[9]

This kind of searching for minute details of celebrities' lives is unhealthy, and probably won't provide the kind of information needed to decide if a particular artist is right for us. While we must deal justly with blatant public sin when it occurs, always making sure we are not searching for a "speck" in someone else's eye while missing the "log" in our own (Matt. 7:3), we must be careful not to judge one another improperly, or to destroy another's reputation, always.

---

[9]Chris Willman, "Leon Patillo and Philip Bailey," *Contemporary Christian* (10/85), p. 28.

We must also remember the Bible portrays God's people in their triumphs *and* failures. Grace abounded to them, as it does to us. So just as businessmen, preachers and parents sometimes fail, artists fail, too. Castigating Christian artists for their faults has no positive effect. Instead, we need to develop the attitude Christ suggested when the scribes and the Pharisees asked Him if they should punish a woman caught in the act of adultery: "Let him who is without sin among you be the first to throw a stone at her" (John 8:7, RSV). In other words, let's be loving and sensitive when we deal with discernment of another's life, remembering there's a difference between discerning and judging. Though it's scriptural to judge when a Christian falls into serious sin, let's temper our judgment with charity.

How then are we to judge Christian contemporary music artists' lifestyles?

Not only must we learn *how* to judge, we also must learn *what* to judge. As music fans, we need to apply the lesson Jesus taught in John 7, when He chided the Pharisees not to "judge by appearances, but judge with right judgment" (John 7:24, RSV). He insisted they look beyond manmade customs and laws and acknowledge the fruit of His ministry.

In the same way, we should look beyond the superficial differences we might have with the way an artist conducts his or her ministry and check for the fruit—both in his life and in the lives of his fans. Who is being touched? In what way does this artist's life and ministry affect others? Are lives being transformed because of this person's public witness? Is the artist "pointing" his life and his performance toward Jesus—giving Jesus the glory and clearly performing in the name of the Lord?

If the answer to those questions is yes, rejoice in that person's gifts and ministry, and don't worry if his lifestyle or music style is one you fail to appreciate. Remember Jesus' answer to His disciples when they told Him some others—not of their group—were casting out demons in the name of the Lord, and they forbade them to continue. Don't forbid them, Jesus admonished, "for no one who does a mighty work in my name will be able soon after to speak evil of me. For he that is not against us is for us." Then Jesus said anyone who serves in His name will be rewarded, but "whoever causes one of these little ones who believe in me to sin, it would be better for him if a great millstone were hung around his neck and he were thrown into the sea" (Mark 9:38–42, RSV).

It is a stern warning. All rock music artists—secular and Christian—must seriously consider the responsibilities they bear, for as Christian performer Robin Crow frankly confessed to music critic Bob Darden, "I've never felt what I've said from the stage has made as big a difference as my daily life."

What is the artist's responsibility to young people?

Having discussed the problems our Christian artists often encounter, and having cautioned against judgmental attitudes, the fact still remains that an artist's public lifestyle can have a powerful impact on his young fans, and rock stars must shoulder the responsibility that comes with the territory. As Melody Green cautions, "Anyone on stage is a role model whether he wants to be or not and whether he acknowledges it or not. That's where the responsibility comes in. It costs."

The cost is totaled in many different ways—lack of privacy, the rigors of road life, the hostility of the media. But perhaps the most difficult for the Christian artist has always been what music critic Paul Baker calls "walking his talk." "The role of the musician often bordered on that of a preacher," Baker says in reference to Christian contemporary music's roots, "and if the musician took that position, he should back-up his words with an active witness in his own behavior."[10]

As mentioned earlier, the writer of James seems to agree with Baker. Though referring to teachers, his warning applies to preachers and artists as well when he says not many should become teachers because they "will be judged with greater strictness than others" (James 3:1, GNB). Writers, preachers, television personalities, musicians, politicians—anyone with a public platform—will be held more accountable because of the influence he possesses.

Furthermore, the writer of James demands these "teachers"

---

[10]Paul Baker, *Contemporary Christian Music* (Westchester, Ill.: Crossway Books, 1985), p. 162.

should be known for their good lives, good works and their humble, compassionate natures, not for their boasting or even for wisdom. He instructs them to search their motives for selfishness and greed, to wait patiently for their ministries to bear fruit, and to not seek rich earthly rewards or luxury.

Why does God ask so much of those in teaching positions? Why must they give so much of themselves? Because it is impossible to separate the music from the man. An artist could conceivably wallow in sin and still write wonderful music. As Kerry Livgren noted before, both Richard Wagner and Claude De-Bussy were known for their ungodly lives, yet much of their music is unsurpassed. So to base the music's worth *solely* on the artist's lifestyle is too simplistic.

However, as Jerusalem's Swedish bassist Peter Carlsson insists, "I don't give a message. I *am* a message. . . . We can sing about Jesus and it can be very empty—a lot of beautiful words, but it just feels cold. Why? Because it's not 'in' the person who is singing; his life is not backing up the words."

In other words, "A good person brings good out of the treasure of good things in his heart; a bad person brings bad out of his treasure of bad things. For the mouth speaks what the heart is full of" (Luke 6:45, GNB). The lifestyle of the performer, then, is often reflected in his music.

Reflecting the Right Treasure

In order to reflect the right "treasure," an artist needs to guard four important relationships: his relationships with God, with his family, with fellow believers, and with his fans.

Mellow songmaster Steve Green agrees that his relationship with God is of utmost importance. "I think it's important for all music people to have music coupled with a secret life of seeking the Lord, finding him, knowing him, and having a deep walk with him. Music is only half of what I do," he adds. "My other half is studying and living with the Lord."

Before his death another Green—Christian artist Keith Green—also spoke of the importance of a relationship with the Lord when living in the public eye: "The only thing I want to represent is the voice of the Lord calling people to live in holiness. The world is tired of religious sayings, they're really dying! They want to see the Gospel lived and Christians have to realize their responsibility to show that life to others."[11]

Private time with the Lord should be a number-one priority, but another "treasure" of any Christian artist should be time spent with his family. It is so important, in fact, that Paul warned Timothy, "If any one does not provide for his relatives, and especially for his own family, he has disowned the faith and is worse than an unbeliever" (1 Tim. 5:8, RSV).

By "providing" Paul refers to more than simply meeting physical needs. He knew anyone in a public position would lose credibility if his family's needs for love, support and guidance were not met. It's difficult to swallow a message about love and commitment sung by a man whose wife is divorcing him, or to hear songs about caring for starving orphans from a woman whose children are love-starved.

Veteran Christian contemporary music producer/agent Wes Yoder maintains, "Other things are more important than what happens on our stages—it's what happens in real life. We in the Christian music industry are so cutesy in explaining away the absolutes of the Gospel, the absolute law of God. Divorce is sanctioned and all sorts of things are explained away. And we think we can have a wonderful ministry. I say that's nonsense."

In addition to the priorities of pursuing God and building family relationships, a Christian in the entertainment field owes it to himself and his fans to develop the treasure of fellowship in a local body. Bill Findlay, of the Canadian-bred Daniel Band, says he uses a priority list, and following his relationship with Jesus and with his family, "fellowship in a local church is absolutely important. If you don't get fellowship in a local church where you are getting your worship, your fellowship and local teaching, then you're going to be a wash-out as a Christian."

Rez Band's Glenn Kaiser agrees: "I would say to any young Christian rock group to make it a top priority to be in a good, Bible-believing, God-fearing, discipling church . . . a church that

---

[11]"Keith Green, Part Three," *New Christian Music* (Vol. 2, No. 1), p. 35.

is involved in your personal life, who can give you guidance as well as correction, who can guide you career-wise and—from a spiritual aspect—keep you on the right track."

One final treasure in a Christian rock star's lifestyle is closeness with people who—as Steve Taylor puts it—"are very unimpressed with Steve Taylor. [People] who know that I'm no big deal and have no problem reminding me!" Taylor is well aware that artists whose days and nights are filled with applause from fans and pats on the back from star struck hangers-on will eventually develop a warped view of their own importance—an attitude that is deathly to Christian ministry.

"There is always the temptation to become proud," observes Christian singer Greg Volz. "I mean self-elation and self-esteem to the extreme that you believe your own press. . . . You become a law unto yourself, and there's no submission in your heart."[12] It's unfortunate to see an artist who gets that "puffed up." His faith-walk as well as his lifestyle and his ministry can go off on a tangent. Even more sad, he sometimes takes his fans with him.

"After being a youth pastor for five years," explains Steve Taylor, "I recognize that kids go through a certain stage where they have got to have heroes, and it's better for them to have heroes in Christian music than to have Twisted Sister or Ozzy Osbourne or whomever. . . . [But] when it gets to a place where kids really stop seeing Jesus," he contends, "then we have a problem."

That's the bottom line when it comes to artists' lifestyles. Hopefully, in everything they do, our Christian rock artists will strive to let Jesus shine through, for if their music fans miss seeing Jesus, they've missed the Treasure the music is all about.

---

[12]Paul Baker, "Must the Show Go On?" *Charisma* (2/86), p. 68.

Chapter Eight

Goals

Perfection of means and confusion of ends seem to characterize our age.

—*Albert Einstein*

All of us have goals—underlying motives for what we do, standards by which we establish our priorities and judge our successes. In the same way, artists have goals, or intentions for their music. Some, undoubtedly, are in it for the glory, the power or the money. Still others are looking for a platform from which to present their views or to offer the answers they have found to life's puzzles.

If you are already a fan of Christian contemporary music, you need to be aware of the goals of the artists you enjoy because the motives for their music affect their message. If you are new to the Christian music scene, knowing each artist's intentions is just as important as learning about his style.

You need not delve into every detail to discover an artist's most personal intentions, but having a feel for his basic goals will help you make a proper match with your musical preferences. After all, each person has different musical tastes. For instance, a 40-year-old mother of two is going to find certain music appealing and useful, while her 13-year-old won't be able to relate to it. Likewise, a street-wise teenager is going to have different tastes and needs than his church-raised contemporaries.

Knowing the motivating forces behind musicians is important if you are to become a good discerner. If a group says its goal is to minister through music, and yet neither song nor stage presentation ever mentions God or calls for commitment or change,

74157

the group is singing under false pretenses. Likewise, if an artist claims his goal is presenting Christ to the unsaved and yet appears only in churches and couches his songs in "church-y" lingo, he may be missing his own mark.

On the following pages, then, you will find the stated goals of a broad cross section of today's contemporary Christian music (CCM) artists. We've tried to include performers from a variety of contemporary styles—middle-of-the-road (MOR) to hard rock to soul—and to describe their sound. We've also attempted to list as many as possible, including some artists who are professed Christians, but choose to perform mainstream music.

To include every performer would, of course, have been impossible. Groups break up or reorganize, and newcomers arrive on the scene almost every day. And to be frank, not all artists take time to clearly formulate and state their goals.

Artists' goals also change. Today, and hopefully tomorrow, an artist might be genuinely singing for the Lord. But human nature as it is, not every artist will always make right choices. To know accurately, we need to follow current information. Occasionally, we may also find it necessary to delve further into the goals of a particular group before deciding if it is appropriate for us. As an aid to such research, the bibliography for this book lists publications that may provide continuing information.

You will soon discover we purposely have not commented on the goals artists have stated for their music, thus allowing their words to speak for themselves. Although, on the whole, we were favorably impressed with the Christian artists we have met and researched, the opinions they express herein do not necessarily reflect our views. Furthermore, inclusion of any group or artist on this list, or anywhere else in this book, should not be construed as support or approval.

We have already provided you with the guidelines to judge music and artists for yourself, and believe you therefore are able to make wise decisions. With no further delay, then, let's survey our Christian musicians—from the mild to the wild—and discover their musical motives.

A.D.: Two former cohorts from the secular band Kansas—Dave

Hope and Kerry Livgren—formed A.D. to sing synth-rock for the Lord. Some critics say A.D.'s searing vocals are among the best in contemporary Christian music. When asked about goals, Hope responds, "With Kansas it was easy: Try to sell a lot of records, make a lot of money, and hold the thing together. In God's work, all those motivations are gone. . . . It'd be great if a revival would break out in front of us, but that's up to God—if we're just seed planters, then that's not going to happen. I'm just here because God wants me here" (Brian Quincy Newcomb, *Contemporary Christian*, 8/85, p. 22).

Says Livgren: "The bottom line is, follow Jesus. I hate to make it a platitude, but it's that simple, just follow Jesus, don't follow men. . . . Dave and I have started at the top and we're working our way down—not the other way around—and it's a very humbling thing. But, boy, is it rich! It's a wonderful thing the Lord's allowed us to do."

Allies: This group—which sounds a bit like Journey or REO— has drafted a military motif, declaring war of a spiritual nature. Former Sweet Comfort Band songwriter and guitarist Randy Thomas states, "I feel Allies can be a positive role model. You can have rock 'n' roll, excitement, high energy and be a Christian."

Vocalist Bob Carlisle adds, "Kids are kids. The energy level that kids have is always going to be there. You can't restrain a kid from having the desire to be a little wild and crazy—but this energy has to be channeled away from Satan" (Scott Pinzon, *Contemporary Christian*, 6/85).

Altar Boys: This self-styled garage band with a simple, gut-level message for both Christians and non-Christians receives both guidance and support from Calvary Chapel of Costa Mesa, Calif. Guitarist, singer and spokesperson Mike Stand explains that Calvary Chapel ensures they keep "the focus in the right place— that we're not taking kids and teaching them how to be Christian punks, but how to be Christians.

"Our goal," adds Stand, "is to bring more young people into a tight relationship with Jesus Christ. Not that the world or the Church needs another Altar Boys to add to its collection, but if

God uses us to do that, then we're more than happy to be a part of it."

Steve Archer: A preacher's kid who was raised in the church, Archer says he, as everyone else, had to come to a place where he admitted he needed the Lord, and now he's telling people what Jesus means to him.

With a positive-pop sound, Archer hopes to reach people anywhere from ten to sixty with a "solid, entertaining, meaty ministry." He explains, "I want to say something to excite people, to challenge them, but also to be fun.

"I'm not the kind of minister that Keith Green—whom I deeply respect—was. I'm more like a spiritual cheerleader. I would say that most of what I do is upbeat and fun" (Scott Pinzon, *Contemporary Christian*, 12/85, p. 22).

Philip Bailey: Bailey, whom the *Los Angeles Times* has called "Earth, Wind and Fire's secret weapon," is quick to point out that he is not quitting mainstream music to enter the Christian field. "I'll continue a dual career, doing Gospel as well as pop records while holding high the Christian standard," Bailey assures.

"My desire," says the soul/pop singer, "is to let my light shine through many kinds of musical expression. I admire the way Bill Cosby has multiple careers as a comedian and as an educator. That's the way I want to approach my ministry. My music, whether secular or Gospel, is a witness. . . . No matter what I'm doing, I want them to see Jesus."

Georgian Banov: Bulgarian-born Banov formed the first official rock band in communist Bulgaria, but when they were banned he escaped in the trunk of a taxi, made his way to the U.S., met the Lord, and later formed the trio Silverwind. Now soloing, Banov declares evangelism—preaching the Gospel—is his primary aim. "People say, 'Why do you sing, why don't you just preach?' We use music to draw people. The heart of the music is to see people come to Christ and to see lives changed. We are not out there touring to promote Christian gospel music; we are there to promote the Lord."

Valeri Barinov: Another communist bloc resident, Valeri Barinov, wrote a Christian rock opera, *The Trumpet Call*, as a way to communicate to Soviet young people. Today, however, he sits in a Soviet labor camp where he endures solitary confinement for sharing the gospel with other inmates. Several religious rights groups are making efforts to bring Barinov's plight to the attention of Soviet premier Mikhail Gorbachev.

Before Barinov's arrest for allegedly trying to cross the Soviet border—a charge he denies—he smuggled out a Russian-language version of *The Trumpet Call*. Solo artist Scott Wesley Brown is distributing that effort on the I Care record label, with English lyrics enclosed. Another artist, Dave Markee, has re-recorded the opera and made it available through Refuge Records.

Peter Beveridge: The child of Christian parents, Australian-born Beveridge proclaims, "My burden for Australia is for the salvation of souls and the discipleship of Christians. There're so many nominal Christians; I would like to see a lot more attention paid to growth in their lives."

Singing a Billy Joel-mixture of jazz rock, rock and roll, and techno-pop, Beveridge plays to a mixed audience: To non-Christians he presents the gospel in a very contemporary way, and to Christians he sends the message, "Share your faith."

"I feel our music has been given to us to communicate the gospel. Our desire should be to learn how to do that more thoroughly, and to be true servants" (Jon Trott, *Cornerstone*, Vol. 10, Issue 58, pp. 38–39).

Debby Boone: Boone, who began her career with the MOR secular sensation, "You Light Up My Life," admits, "It's naive to think you can sing with a real heavy Christian message and expect radio programmers to go ahead and play it—just because you had a hit once." However, she adds that partially due to more professional-sounding songs, Christian records do occasionally get airplay if they offer "a message of truth, but not necessarily religion.

"A lot of my music is going to have a heavy message that isn't for everybody," she stresses, ". . . but along with it, I'm going to try and expand to a larger audience with things that I feel are important to everyone. And hopefully I'll be able to make that work."

Bash-n-the Code: Philadelphia's former Found Free are, according to executive director of Myrrh Records, Lynn Nichols, "visual and outrageous, but, at the same time, very celebrative." Relates Nichols, "Bash aims at the teen and pre-teen market. In the past, we have ignored this age, the one that listens to Duran Duran and Wham! . . . My kids tell me that Christian music is not visual enough. Bash fills this void."

According to lead singer Rebecca Ed Sparks, Bash wants a party-like, energetic atmosphere at their concerts, but they also want to communicate God's comforting love to teens who, as Sparks did, find their teen years very scary.

Scott Wesley Brown: "I do admit there are a lot of people playing Star Games," says veteran Christian MOR composer/ministrel Scott Wesley Brown, "and there's a lot of competition . . . [but] people need to know that because of lack of support and guidance by the local churches (which need to be involved in contemporary Christian music), a lot of artists are really fighting to keep their ministries alive" (Jon Trott, *Cornerstone,* Vol. 10, Issue 54, p. 39).

Brown's own ministry spans the globe, and he has shared his easy-listening ballads and pop-rock tunes all over Europe and Russia, as well as the U.S. About his goals, Brown asserts, "There are four purposes to music in the Bible: praise, fellowship, communication and confession. That's where our concerns should lie. Of course, through that we have the potential to entertain, but it really goes much deeper" (*Contemporary Christian,* 2/82, p. D-14).

Steve Camp: Sharp-edged rocker Steve Camp produces intense, complex lyrics concerned with issues both personal and global. On one record sleeve, the self-described gospel communicator writes, "I have felt the sting of compromise too real in my life. Have you also? . . . We need to repent my friend. . . . It's a desperate hour we live in that needs disciplined, dynamic, sold-out Christians to be examples to a lost world and a lukewarm church."

It is a theme which permeates his music and he sees his musical career as a vocation in the same sense as 2 Timothy 2:2. Says Camp: "I hope what I can do in this art form of music will not only make a difference for this year but the results will far outlive myself. . . . I wanna be a servant. I want to know what it is to wash feet . . . smelly feet, ugly feet, old wrinkled feet. . . . I need to understand what it is to serve and if that's through music—then wonderful!" (Paul Davis, *New Christian Media*, 11–12/85, p. 32).

Michael Card: With his radically Christ-centered lyrics and his timeless ballads, Card doesn't easily fit any category of contemporary music, but his tunes are reminiscent of Dan Fogelberg's folk-pop styling. "I thought God wanted me to be a teacher," Michael notes. "As it ends up, I do teach—in a different sense—but it's still teaching. What I've always wanted to do is to get people interested in reading the Bible."

"My songs are interpretations of the Bible," Card explains. "What I try to do is to interact with whatever text it is based on—interact with my imagination and try to fill things out. You've got to make the message your own somehow."

Pete Carlson: Strong, honest lyrical content dominates the distinctive jazz/pop tunes of performer and songwriter Pete Carlson. Carlson confesses, however, his original intentions were less than ideal. "To be very honest, I don't think in the very beginning my motives were as pure as what they should have been or what everybody thought they were. I was drawn into music the way a lot of kids are, because they see the glamour, the attention, the travel, the opportunities that are afforded musicians."

However, when the bright lights paled, he reassessed his motivation. Carlson's Al Jarreau-like stylings are now aimed at "giving a balanced look at Christianity—the whole picture—that we are human beings with frailties. My motive is to share Jesus Christ through my music from a very personal standpoint. . . . not a 'misery loves company' approach, but letting people know they are not alone in their struggle."

Carman: Carman, who quips he dropped his last name, Licciardello, because if he used it in some churches, "they'd ask for an interpretation," is a mesmerizing storyteller with a street-wise Las Vegas style. "Everything I have to contribute is right there on stage," he affirms. "The message is Jesus Christ, and I try to deliver it with as much universality and power as I can, because that's where He's at."

The MOR showman says he tries to cover several bases in his music: a contemporary style for teens, biblically authoritative ideas for mature Christians, modern themes and concerns to interest the unsaved, and lots of humor for all. "Humor is an important part of my act," says Carman. "It lets people know that there is joy in being a Christian."

Paul Clark: Reaching out to the street where he came from is the personal challenge of Paul Clark, whose history in Christian music dates back to 1971. With jazz-rock, keyboard-oriented music, Clark aims for what he calls "cutting edge Christian music." "Though there is a definite place for entertaining Christians," he says, "my main burden is reaching out to the lost. I don't want to limit myself to playing Christian 'Bless me' concerts. There's a real difference between true evangelism and entertaining Christians." As a result, Clark has formed a nonprofit organization, Paul Clark Ministries, which he uses to subsidize concerts in small towns, prisons, and colleges.

Billy Crockett: A dynamic vocalist, able acoustic guitarist and passionate lyricist, Crockett is described by his press material as "a fresh new sound." According to Word Records, his songs (which belie a Latin influence) have two main goals: to show God's love as "an explosive force in our society" and to express honestly God's loving acceptance of our humanness and failure: "The only way any of us can open ourselves up to the love of God is by being fallible . . . broken vessels."

Robin Crow: A Christian "underground" artist who plays secular venues 99 percent of the time, Crow maintains, "I feel I'm supposed to play in places where I can attract a cross section of people. If you shine for God, people know it."

Though his songs are filled with Christian expressions of love and joy, they have been successful mainly outside the Christian sphere and Crow is not certain most Christian labels are ready for his philosophy. "There are artists who do nothing but play praise music for believers," he says. "Great. My music is not praise or evangelism. I don't even call it a ministry, because that puts a hundred expectations on you before you ever play a note" (Bob Darden, *Contemporary Christian*, 8/83, p. 28).

Crumbacher: Borrowing from the new wave and pop influences of the late seventies, this California-based group delivers rapid-fire, straightforward messages designed to speak to the relevant issues of the day—humanism, situation ethics, materialism—but in a catchy, up-tempo way. Steve Crumbacher, the group's founder, confides, "Basically, the reason I'm in this is because I love music. And the reason I'm doing it for the Lord is because I love the Lord." The handsome lead vocalist adds, "I don't really separate my music and my walk with God. I want everything I do to be colored with Christlikeness so that—no matter what I'm doing—others will know my main goal is to serve God."

Keyboardist Dawn Wisner-Johnson says the group especially identifies with church kids, because they all grew up in the church. "A lot of kids come to where they just turn off because they've heard it so many times before, it no longer means anything. And we can understand the feeling of wanting to go out and experience the world, of doing what your friends are doing, and yet we know what we have—the Lord—is really the best."

The Cruse: Formerly a family-founded, gospel group, Joe—the oldest brother—and two sisters, Cindy and Karen, have spun off into a keyboard-dominated pop-rock style. They stress, however, that their message is still the same: Christ's life-saving power. "We're trying to get a hold of those kids who have not been saved, and we want to go out there where they are and use the type of music they listen to," says Joe Cruse.

"We're going into some places where they've never allowed Christian music to come and we share in that form," Cruse adds, noting their successes on college campuses. "It's exciting because we have a tool they accept and they can grab hold of, and they listen to what we have to say."

Morgan Cryar: "The problem I see in the younger generation is a basic mistrust of God," says high-energy rocker Morgan Cryar. "They really don't believe in their deepest heart that God is safe. They're nervous about giving Him charge of their lives."

"As I see it," the young artist told *Christian Activities Calendar*, "my job is to use any influence I have with the kids to convince them of the ultimate trustworthiness of God. . . . My passion is simply to see young people (Christians and non-Christians) give their lives to God, believe that he is determined to make them the most joyful people on earth" (11–12/85, p. 15).

Rick Cua: A seasoned rocker in the traditional sense, who speaks to both saved and unsaved, is former Outlaw band member Rick Cua. Cua declares, "I'm a musician. Music is a career to me; it's how I pay my bills. And I want to reach people that would appreciate it. But it's not a ministry in the sense of 'Send to Rick Cua Ministries.' I believe that if I lead a Christian life, and the Lord lives in me—as I know He does—then I am going to minister, just as every Christian ministers whether he likes it or not."

"My songs," Cua admits, "as blunt as they are to me, aren't always as blunt to other people. I don't write about Jesus in every single song." However, he's quick to add, "There are certainly strong messages in every song, a lot of seeds going down. I'm not saying they'll be used for a gigantic altar call in Madison Square Garden, but they plant seeds and draw people closer. . . . There's more than one way to win the world over for Christ."

Daniel Amos Band: Terry Taylor, Daniel Amos Band's innovative lead vocalist, points out, "There are some people God has called to evangelism and they're doing a wonderful job, having results. That's great." However, the outspoken chief lyricist reveals he felt trapped into having to validate the existence of his new music, bizarro-wave band by displaying spiritual results, what he calls "fast food evangelism."

"God wanted us to do something else," he goes on, "so we got into the area of challenging people, and our ministry basically happens offstage—one-on-one—when we talk with people. It's very subtle, but God's doing a work! It's entertainment, it's fun, it's a concert—it's all those things—but at a subtle, deeper level, it touches people's hearts."

Daniel Band: With a focus on no-holds-barred evangelism, this Canadian band dispenses loud, no-frills rock and roll in the Rush or Triumph vein. "People will respect you if you go all out and give them a good product musically, and tell them what you really believe," declares guitarist Bill Findlay. "People will want to respect you for standing up for what you think is right. I see a lot of wishy-washy Christian musicians, and it really upsets me that they would try to gloss over the message."

Still, Daniel Band insists its fans will receive from their concerts only if they "come to a concert with an open heart, expecting not just to have a great time and 'rock on,' but to learn something or to be encouraged. . . . If they come with an open mind and open heart, they'll receive it."

Darrell Mansfield Band: Hard rock with a bluesy edge best describes this band's style, and up-front evangelism describes their motives. There is time for prayer and commitment at each performance, and members of the group come out front and talk with fans after the show. The driving force of the group, Darrell Mansfield, emphasizes, "If you're gonna really be out there, in front of all those people and you've got an audience, then you should be making the most of that. . . . I've been trying for years to break this thing open and let people see there's a validity to ministering through rock 'n' roll," he insists. "All we're trying to do is be 'all things to all people.' We're trying to be bait on the hook—Jesus is the hook, we're the bait" (Mike Hertenstein, *Cornerstone*, Vol. 13, Issue 73, p. 49).

David and the Giants: Originally a secular group formed in the early seventies, all four members of the group once struggled with drugs. By 1979, their lives turned around by a newfound faith, the group had shifted from secular rock to performing contemporary Christian music. Stylistically, they now are back to their Southern rock and roll roots. However, they say their goal is to infuse their songs with strong statements of faith, trust in Christ, and encouragement to take everything—whether hardship or victory—in stride when walking with the Lord.

DeGarmo and Key: "We will always try to communicate our faith and the Gospel to both believers and nonbelievers in the most contemporary music language available to us," claims Dana Key, of the streamlined rock duo which has been exploring music together since meeting in grade school.

Though they have met many obstacles, their determination to use rock as a sharing tool has paid off. They were the first Christian rock group to receive a Grammy nomination and to have a concept video aired on MTV. Key explains his motivation: "I didn't want to cram anything down anybody's throat, but I did have to share what Jesus had done in my life. I had to! Not that I minded; it was my pleasure. I had made a commitment to God that I would never play if I couldn't get that across."

Teri De Sario: A unique pop vocalist, as at home with rock as with disco, country and blues, De Sario offers variety in both style and content. She writes most of her own lyrics, which are compelling but controversial, yet her goals are quite traditional: "I'm called to love others with the love that He loved me," she relates.

"I believe in a down-to-earth, compassionate approach to the Gospel," she revealed to *Contemporary Christian* magazine. "I think we need to talk to people on their level and in everyday terms about Jesus. The Christian life is not a bunch of do's and don'ts, but a life of what you can accomplish in Christ" (5/86, p. 14).

Dion: By the time Dion DiMucci was 17, he and the Belmonts had a million-selling record, "Teenager in Love." But with the success came alcohol and drug abuse. In 1979, though, Dion asked Jesus Christ into his life and he says the Lord "turned me around 180 degrees."

Since expanding musically into reggae, blues and rock, Dion's songwriting goals have expanded as well. "I feel like I am starting to see God as a loving and encouraging God, concerned more with progress than perfection," he asserts. "When I first started playing my Christian music, I would go out waving my finger and telling people what they had to do. . . . I guess that's OK—that's where I was then. But today I'm learning to be a little more honest and to do what's comfortable. My ministry today is based on encouragement, not fear."

Jessy Dixon: Dixon, a seasoned performer of music ranging from gospel to jazz, from soulful pop to rock, became a Christian in 1972. Since then he has held concerts in prestigious Carnegie Hall and Madison Square Garden, produced numerous gold albums and received repeated Grammy nominations.

Despite the recognition, however, Dixon attempts to point to God as his source. "I used to think it was talent, or a suit, or the way I walked on stage, or how I hit a high note that brought them to their feet at a concert," he confesses. "Now I don't even try to make the audience relate to me. I just keep pointing to Jesus" (Sally Parker, *Religious Broadcasting*, 2/86, p. 60).

Phil Driscoll: Driscoll's powerful, gravelly vocals, and jazzy, sweet trumpet playing have been ministering to people since 1968. "Praise has always been the most effective music for me," Driscoll explained to an interviewer following one sold-out performance. However, his skill elicits support from soul, pop, rock and jazz lovers, as well as more traditional music fans.

"As I get more involved in the ministry," he notes, "I'm becoming more aware of the need to minister outside the Body of Christ. If I'm performing in a prison, for example, most of what I do there is just that—perform. I may only minister verbally for five or ten minutes, because I need to get those people in the frame of mind to want to listen to me, by playing the type of music that they're used to hearing. I am trying to keep my craft at a level that will allow me to flow with the Holy Spirit" (Paul Baker, *Christian Activities Calendar*, 11–12/85, p. 5).

Roby Duke: A Mississippi boy who, as early as age 13, played in secular bands, Duke credits his mother with praying him through to salvation. From that point on, he's been singing for the Lord. "Only due to my relationship with God and God's nurturing in my life, am I at all creative," he concedes. "It's all because of God, for God. So it must communicate God."

In the pop tradition of Christopher Cross, Duke offers ballad-stories about life. "All of my music that people come to see me perform has been fruits of heart changes—things I actually feel."

Bryan Duncan: After years with Sweet Comfort Band, Duncan says a solo ministry is less distracting, making goal-setting easier. His music, which he describes as "up-sound, danceable pop," now handles heavy issues such as holiness and commitment, with a light hand. "I want to enjoy myself, not take myself so seriously," he explains. "But, even more, I just want to follow the Lord and see where He leads."

What brought the lighthearted change? After Sweet Comfort, Duncan says, he had to "recommit to the Lord. I was kind of surprised to realize that God loves me, too. . . . I've discovered the joy of salvation" (Scott Pinzon, *Contemporary Christian*, 8/85, p. 14).

Bob Dylan: In 1981, the controversial folk-rock troubador was quoted by *Cornerstone* magazine: "I just have to hope that in some kind of way this music that I've always played is a healing kind of music. If it isn't, I don't want to do it. . . . If I can't do something that is telling people, or hoping anyway, that whatever their sickness is (and we're all sick), they can be healed and well and set straight, if I can't do that, I'd just as soon be on a boat, I'd just as soon be off hiking through the woods" (Vol. 10, Issue 56).

Should Christians tell Dylan to "take a hike"? It's a very personal choice, made more difficult since he has stamped his lost-and-found faith "top secret," and not felt the need to provide his fans with a yearly spiritual health report. "People want to know where I'm at because they don't know where they're at," he insists.

Dave Edwards Band: New wave, pop-oriented sounds, and meaningful, somewhat unconventional lyrics have been Edwards' personal stamp since 1971. Edwards says his desire is to follow God's will, not to sell records: "My goal is to be as close with God as possible and to do what he wants me to do. And in order to be that way, I shouldn't have preferences as to how that would be answered; in other words, if God did want me to go back to computer programming it shouldn't make any difference."

Citing models such as C. S. Lewis and George MacDonald, Edwards prefers honesty, pure and simple: "When it comes to writing, I try to be myself. I don't think it takes some 'higher perception.' All it takes is being human" (*Cornerstone*, Vol. 13, Issue 71, p. 42).

ēlim Hall: Canada's ēlim Hall—named after a church where the trio's families have their roots—offer tight vocal harmonies, raw, driving percussion, and lyrics written in the language of today's youth.

Explains the youngest member of the group, guitarist Glen Teeple, "I think we're young enough, and maybe naive enough, to believe that we can really make a difference in the world, and I think people are drawn to that" (*Contemporary Christian*, 4/86, p. 12).

The English Band: With former Wings drummer Joe English navigating, this contemporary rock group plans to touch young lives. Offers English, "We share testimony, scripture, and most of all we're open to let the Lord lead at each concert. We try to let people know that Christ is real—that they can go to Him and He will hear their prayers. Many of the kids that come to our concerts are already born again, but they don't realize the personal relationship with Christ is so important. That's what we're trying to convey."

Eternity Express: Ken Gaub pioneered Youth Outreach Unlimited ministry over 30 years ago, and now it includes a 24-hour "hot line," a prison ministry, mission support, motivational seminars and a five-member, full-time rock group—Eternity Express.

"Music is the most powerful medium in the world," Gaub insists. "If music can be tapped to tell people about Jesus, I feel that it has even more effect than Christian television." Gaub adds, "We will keep on doing what we are doing, just as long as we can continue to have a positive impact on lives through our live appearances and albums" (*Christian Activities Calendar*, 11–12/85, p. 18).

Farrell and Farrell: Bob and Jayne Farrell have been touching their audiences with both soft ballad and driving beat for more than 15 years. The couple's hope is to dispel with their highly-refined synthesizer music, the "spiritual giant" syndrome promoted by some Christian musicians and television evangelists. "Our pride, everybody's pride, keeps us from wanting the rest of the world to know that we have faults," theorizes Jayne Farrell. However, they desire to be vulnerable, transparent. "I want these people to see us, to know that we are real, too, that we have problems" (Bob Darden, *Contemporary Christian*, 9/84, p. 20).

John Fischer: In an industry that is less than 20 years old, John Fischer stands out as a patriarch of sorts. "God can use anyone who is willing to be used," he once told *Bookstore Journal.* The pioneer folk-rock performer likes to put his ministry—and his life—in the biblical framework of Colossians 3:16: "Let the Word of Christ richly dwell within you; with all wisdom teaching and admonishing one another with psalms and hymns and spiritual songs, singing with thankfulness in your hearts to God" (NASB).

"That became the cornerstone for what I wanted to build and continues to be so," Fischer concludes. "First, that we have something dwelling in us, the Word, the Spirit of Christ. And secondly, that we are prepared not just musically, but prepared spiritually" (*Cornerstone*, Vol. 12, Issue 65, p. 38).

Don Francisco: A premiere parable-teller, Don Francisco, feels his strongest call is to Christians who may never know there's much more to Christian life "unless they see or hear or feel it in a concert setting. It's at that point that they're able to receive something from God they never knew existed."

The guitarist who uses painful experiences from his own life to encourage others to seek healing, adds, "My thrust is still holiness. I really want God to use me to help bring about revival. I don't know how he's going to do it, but I do know that revival first has to happen within me and I pray for it earnestly every day."

Tom Franzak: Frustrated by the lack of positive music available for his church choir, Franzak set out to write music that "would minister to basic problems." Now he has a special ministry to young people, creating songs that meet specific needs.

"I don't think people need just to hear that Jesus died for me. They need to be told what that means when they roll out of bed and face another day." That's where Franzak hopes his Billy Joel-type tunes come in: "Address an issue in a straightforward way and those kids listen. What a great tool music can be!"

R. K. Fraser: As a member of the California State Board of the American Coalition of Traditional Values, singer and songwriter R. K. Fraser's goal is to see America "get back to the basics." His music, full of patriotism, heroes and "the dignity of self that comes with the love of God," calls America to return to the moral principles on which it was founded (*Contemporary Christian*, 3/86, p. 14).

Rob Frazier: A former member of the band Petra, in 1980 Frazier struck out on his own, as a songwriter and producer, and then into a solo music ministry. He believes in enjoying a solid rock and roll style, but he also believes he has a calling. "It's a constant struggle trying to make a living, and the temptation is sometimes there to go for the easy lick," says Frazier. "But first and foremost, our goal is ministry, and we're trying to impact people's lives for the positive—spiritually. We want people to grow in Christ by what we're singing and we're saying. And if they don't know Christ," the Philadelphia native adds, "we want them to see Him through what we're doing."

The Front: "We felt like writing about God," declares co-founder of The Front, Tommy Funderburk, "and we didn't want to do quasi-Christian, read-between-the-lines lyrics. We didn't want to have to rely on capital H's." With vocals reminiscent of Journey's Steve Perry, the pop-rock-jazz group dispenses gut-level lyrics about today's hottest issues in secular venues where most Christian bands don't stand a chance.

"Many times people have said we're blowing our careers by doing this," Funderburk admits. "But God has called me to do it. I think the church has done a pretty efficient job of burning all the bridges and hiding out. I think it's time we started claiming back some credibility" (Scott Pinzon, *Contemporary Christian*, 6/85, p. 31).

Amy Grant: In an exclusive *Bookstore Journal* interview, Grant told writer Liz Gilland, "If someone is trying to figure out what my ministry is—although I don't use the word 'ministry'—I'd say that God has used the aims I have for my personal life and allowed me to communicate them to thousands of people. My message, essentially, is 'Get to know Him.' "

Her uncomfortableness with the word 'ministry,' Grant says, stems from her observation that the church often "compartmentalizes" activities, giving some added, though undeserved attention. When asked what she hopes non-Christians gain from her music, Grant revealed three goals: First, that non-Christians would see that Christianity is not "archaic" but vibrant and thriving. Second, that God is "accessible" and to "whet people's appetite for the Bible." And finally, to show non-Christians that "desiring a relationship with God can be the goal of a thinking man or woman" (7/86, pp. 21–22).

Al Green: A decade ago he was known as the Prince of Love, but today, he's the Rev. Al Green, a Full Gospel Tabernacle minister as well as a pop-gospel singer. His message now, he says, is about the love of the Lord. "My music has to be eternal, [about] everlasting love," Green maintains. "You can't sing about temporal things. I'm not permitted to sing pop music anymore like, 'Baby, baby, you turn me on' " (*Newsweek*, 1/20/86, p. 68A).

Glen Allen Green: A multi-talented singer and songwriter, Texas-born Glen Allen Green is the son of a Baptist minister and a former youth pastor himself. His musical call is bold evangelism. "I want my music to be readily accepted by those outside the church," says Green. "I want those people who are lost to listen to my songs and like them for their art, then let that art lead them to the realization of the Lord" (*Christian Activities Calendar*, Fall-Winter/85, p. 34).

Keith Green: Though this seminal Christian artist died in a plane crash in 1982, his music lives on. Likewise, the balladeer's opinions concerning contemporary Christian music are still valid. In a hand-out entitled "Can God Use Rock Music?" Green wrote, "I am convinced that the potential of reaching people for Jesus through the media—whether it be records, radio, movies, or television—is monumental, simply because these are the things that have, and continue to hold, people's attention. I truly believe that Christians who are completely sold out to God, using these tools, can bring people to their knees in repentance and lead them into the waiting arms of the Savior.

"But if their lives are *not* sold out," the artist cautioned, "if their motives are mixed, and their hearts divided, then I only see ridicule and shame brought to the gospel" (Keith Green, "Can God Use Rock Music?", © 1982, Pretty Good Printing, Last Days Ministries, Box 40, Lindale, TX 75771).

Steve Green: A former Gaithers backup vocalist, as well as a member of both The Gaither Vocal Band and WhiteHeart, Steve Green is now communicating musically as a solo performer. Green says, in order to minister Christ, an artist has to know Him because "people will be ministered to as the life of Christ flows out of me." A primary goal of this middle-of-the-road artist is to "present Christ clearly, boldly, and effectively through music so people can be drawn to Him" (*MusicLine*, 12/85, pp. 9, 10).

Pam Mark Hall: Since recording her first album in 1974, Hall has taken her music from folk to laid-back contemporary rock. Insists Hall, of Christian music, "The subject matter does not make it a Christian song. The fact that I'm Christian and I'm writing from that frame of reference makes it a Christian song." The singer and songwriter sees it as her duty to write about a variety of subjects because Jesus Christ is concerned with and involved in every aspect of life. "I feel it is my responsibility to live life, to let God speak to me, and then to deliver what I have learned through my experiences, through the Word, and through the Holy Spirit" (*MusicLine*, 1/86, p. 12).

Larnelle Harris: Soulfully stunning pop artist Larnelle Harris uses music "as a vehicle to infect people's lives, to change them, to cause them to think about who they are." His vision is to perform music with a lasting quality, songs that are not here today, gone tomorrow: "Trends will last for a while, but the things that are going to be glued to the wall are going to be more than sermons and songs about how to make cakes. There has to be some meat there" (*MusicLine*, 10/85 p. 11).

Harvest: The group's stirring vocals and tight harmonies complement Harvest's bold intentions. Explains Jerry Williams— one-half of the duo, "God has called Harvest and is sending us as watchmen to the church of America. We're consumed with the reality that not many American 'Christians' will enter the kingdom of God." Williams adds their primary goal is to present the "compelling reality" of the spiritual weakness, ineffectiveness and compromised attitudes prevalent in the church today.

Mark Heard: Philosophical, intellectual, esoteric—even cynical— but always with an underlying faith Mark Heard tracks and attacks man's folly. His skillful way with both lyrics and music has made him a favorite with those seeking unadulterated truth in their music.

With a style somewhere between Bob Dylan and James Taylor, Heard strives for what he calls "the human touch." "We need to be concerned about being real, honest people, not haughty and pious; we should begin to stop writing things that are supposedly 'spiritual' and contain all the terminology and intimations of songs that have been written throughout Christian history. We need to move on from where we are and make our faith real in the eyes of the people round us, taking off our masks and letting them see that ours are human faces as well" (*New Christian Media*, Vol. 8, Issue 4, p. 31).

Benny Hester: When Hester first became a Christian, he dropped his rock roots and adopted a sensitive ballad style. However, more recently, he has reverted to high-energy rock and roll. He reasons that rock is more immediate and passionate, and he has some passionate things to say: "I love the Lord so intensely that the intensity has to come out or I'll explode! . . . I did a lot of praying and thinking about what the Lord wanted and how He had best suited me to communicate. I came to the conclusion I needed to go back to what I do best: simple, solid rock, firmly based on The Rock."

Kyle Henderson: Formerly with the Atlanta-based secular group

The Producers, Henderson was never comfortable with the typical rock lifestyle, so he started looking for answers as he observed his friends, his band and his marriage disintegrate. Since his conversion, Henderson's goal has been to reach out to others still soul-searching.

"I'd really like God to use this music as an instrument to touch the hearts of the people from whence I came," the Bryan Adams sound-alike offers. "In other words, the people whom I love and whom we call 'nice people,' my friends from the old days" (*Christian Activities Calendar*, 12/85).

Garth Hewitt: England's swashbuckling musical crusader against social injustice and world hunger uses a variety of musical styles, from bluesy gospel, to samba rhythms, to all-out rock. One goal of the many-faceted artist is to give hope to the hopeless. Hewitt feels many so-called realistic songs point out the negative situation but give no hope. "God draws us out to our full potential," he says. "He offers hope as He helps us understand ourselves. . . . Be realistic, but more than that see the spiritual resources available to us as Christians" (*New Christian Media*, Vol. 2, Issue 9, p. 24).

Dallas Holm and Praise: Hailed as one of CCM's most influential songwriters and singers, Holm's most recent work has leaned toward a heavier rock style, appealing to younger tastes. And yet, his goals remain the same. "Gospel music is more than entertainment," Holm emphasizes. "What's the use of something like this if Jesus doesn't touch lives?"

"With all the tough issues young people face today," Holm adds, ". . . we can use music to communicate godly principles, communicate morals, answers to problems—and we certainly should be. Without being too negative, I think it has been to some degree a failure in Christian music. We've answered all kinds of questions nobody was asking. We've said all kinds of things that really weren't hitting the issues." Holm's goal is to be more issues-oriented, instead of always singing "about the golden streets and the pearly gates. . . . I have got to address all issues. Jesus did."

The Imperials: Their over-riding musical goal, reveal the Imperials, is to remain innovators—at the forefront of Christian pop music. But the spiritual force of their ministry is to end each concert with a brief period of evangelism and a call to commitment or rededication. "Our intention is twofold," the group clarifies. "First, we're a ministry of encouragement to the different segments of the church. Secondly, to the nonbeliever, we have a message—Jesus—and an opportunity to make a decision for Him."

In 3D: This band blasts away at conventional Christian music with searing sounds reminiscent of The Police, and thought-provoking lyrics intended to be question-raisers. Their artful music is representative of a growing volume of Christian rock much like U2's, using an indirect approach to evangelism, asking questions about moral issues and the meaning of life, but not necessarily spoon-feeding easy answers. The Chicago-based wave-metal combo explains, "It's been said that art is not meant to answer questions, but to ask them."

Jerusalem: This group exports rock-style music—hard and heavy—from Sweden to the world. Their insistent, driving melodies make them CCM's answer to Scorpion. It is the culmination of a vision given to the group's lead vocalist, Ulfe Christensson, over 10 years ago when they were playing in small churches and practicing in a tiny cellar. "When we started," he recalls, "God told me we were going to play in the whole world, not only Sweden, with the message God has given us."

Searching emotionally for the right words, Christensson adds, "We have to show this world the power of God—the power, and the glory, and the . . . I can't put it into this language . . . the charisma. If we don't go, who will? Our command is to go into the world and preach the Gospel."

William Harvey Jett: A former member of Black Oak Arkansas, Jett says he thought electric music was "of the Devil" when he first got saved because he had seen it misused so terribly. Then, he says, he felt the Lord was telling him, "You don't think I can bless it, but I can. If you do it for me with the right attitude, I can bless it." Now Jett uses his music to reach out to young people. "The vision I feel now," he volunteers, "is to go to the people that I relate to in the high schools, prisons, street concerts, in the parks. I've got a message, and some music and I'm just waiting on the Lord."

Martyn Joseph: Though a relatively new Christian performer, Joseph has become a major attraction on the U.K. scene, with his unique brand of exuberant pop-rock, as well as his impassioned preaching. "I'm involved in music because I want to communicate—above all else—the reality I've found in being a Christian," Joseph claims. "I'm involved in music because I couldn't stand up with a Bible and preach. . . . I'm in it because it's the best way I've ever come across to express myself personally as a Christian and tell people about my faith" (*New Christian Media*, 5–6/86, p. 34).

Phil Keaggy: Confused by drug abuse, the rock lifestyle, and his mother's early death, Phil Keaggy, formerly of the secular group Glass Harp, did some long overdue soul-searching and gave his life to the Lord. Since then, his virtuoso guitar playing has rightfully earned him a master's title, but he says praise and applause are not his goals: "To me a successful concert is when you know that something penetrated a hardened heart and got through to someone who had a real need, and all of a sudden it seemed to cease to be a concert" (Foster Braun, *Windstorm*, 7–8/83, p. 47).

Brent Lamb: With a successful track record of several hit pop tunes as a writer, Lamb is now pursuing a solo career. Because of problems he encountered as a teenager, Lamb feels he has a strong message for young people, and can truly understand their needs. Brent says his long-range goal is to one day have land for a home, concert house and camp for underprivileged children and teenagers to enjoy Christian concerts and fellowship.

Lenny LeBlanc: Though a successful secular music career seemed within reach, LeBlanc reached a point where he no longer felt the desire to perform music that didn't uplift the Lord. Now he feels one of the primary purposes for music is "to share the gospel with other people. If somebody hadn't shared the gospel with me," he adds, "I'd still be in the world. . . . I feel it's my responsibility to share with others . . . to preach the gospel . . . not to try to be a superstar."

Mylon Le Fevre and Broken Heart: Multi-talented hard-rocker Mylon Le Fevre worked with almost every major rock figure in the seventies, from Eric Clapton to the Allman Brothers, whom his work sometimes sounds like. Since his last secular concert in 1978, he has devoted his life—and music—to the Lord.

Le Fevre maintains, "Kids who will listen to no sermon will listen to good music—and frequently get saved—when hard-hitting sermons are entwined into the lyrics. We're in a spiritual war," insists Le Fevre. "We're competing against [non-Christian] groups like AC/DC, Judas Priest, and Van Halen for the minds and souls of young people. We're seeing thousands come to Christ" (*Charisma*, 2/85, pp. 22–28).

Angie Lewis: A petite dynamo with a big voice and a belief God wants her singing Christian music, Lewis came to Nashville only a few short years ago. She has a growing concern for 18- to 30-year-olds, saved and unsaved, who "run into problems and don't know what to do."

Though she has a voice and style similar to an early Joan Baez or a reborn Sheena Easton, this native Alabaman's motives are far from Easton's shoddy goals: "Whereas some secular artists simply record songs and don't think about the lyrics, I *do* think about my music. I want my songs to have healing messages, or messages of love, or to be songs that say, 'Hey, I've been there too, and here's what I did—here's what I think you should do.' I want to give healing, self-improvement, encouragement."

Lone Justice: A young band with a relatively slick rock-soul-country blend of sounds, Lone Justice is a secular band whose lead vocalist and songwriter, Maria McKee, is a professing Christian. McKee's gritty-sweet vocals cover topics most secular bands never touch. "I think God gives me my songs," she told *Rolling Stone* magazine. "The songs usually just come to me when I pray. None of my songs preach, but I hope some of them have messages of hope and a positive attitude. I think that's important in music, because there's been so much negativity in rock and roll, and sadness. A certain amount of pain in music is wonderful, but you ought to have a certain amount of light and hope, too" (*Rolling Stone*, 7/4 1985, pp. 16–17).

Howard McCrary: A veteran secular music session worker, McCrary feels God has shielded him from much of the evil in mainstream rock. However, he has had to turn down offers which he felt were "lewd and crude." Though he intends to keep doing secular work, the pop singer says his soul is in Christian music, and he wants to reach young people with messages of hope: "I love to perform. I like to physically touch people in the audience. I don't like being distant from them, especially young people. Man, I feel for young people today."

Barry McGuire: In 1965 he recorded "Eve of Destruction," often tagged the theme song of a generation. From there he went to Broadway where he played the male lead in the outrageous musical "Hair." Finally, in a desperate search for truth, he found Jesus. Now he spends most of his energy working with missions in Asia and being "a husband and a daddy," but he still does two short tours of the U.S. each year. His message, he says, is simple truth, stressing "learning to trust God for everything, to cease from our striving" (*Christian Life*, 11/85, p. 48).

Kenny Marks: Kenny Marks sees himself as an artist who can lock onto some of the real issues affecting teenagers today. "I want my music to cut through the sediment and the tough stuff kids are living under today." Marks does so with hard-rocking energy as well as sympathetic understanding.

He sees today's contemporary music as a powerful medicine and says his prayer is, "Lord, take this music, take this energy, take this guitar, take these songs, and turn them for good. And speak to an issue that needs to be spoken to."

David Martin: As both a mainstream and a Christian pop song-writer, Martin's career has been in full gear for some time, though he is now focusing on a solo career. His light rock tunes usually deal in areas of trust, prayer and God's love.

His goal is to communicate "that God is greater than anything we're ever going to figure out or even know. I'd like to go out and spread a feeling of hope through my songs and my singing. I like people to leave my concert thinking, 'What is it that I do that God wants to use—something I'm good at?' God is so great and I think He wants great things for each of us," says Martin.

David Meece: From the Peabody Conservatory of Music, and solo performances with Andre Previn, to power-pop Christian rock, David Meece continues to unleash his creativity and talent along with a message of forgiveness. Notes Meece, "Whatever we have done in our past, we don't need to walk around with a guilt trip. Christ is positive. He said, let's not look upon the past, let's look forward to the future. For those who ask His forgiveness, He is willing to do just that. . . . And that conceptual idea to me is just a marvelous, uplifting, and encouraging thing."

Ken Medema: From Stevie Wonder-style easy-listening ballads, to Harry Chapin-sounding social commentary folk-rock, blind Ken Medema sings songs about values, about war, about friends. However, he feels his most valuable work takes place offstage: "I think I serve an even more important service asking questions (of my hosts) like 'Where is your church going?' or 'Where are the people you are trying to reach?' . . . Then after the performance, it's just as important to go out again and talk about what's been said and sung. A concert is really just an excuse to get together" (Bob Darden, *Charisma*, 2/86, p. 76).

Messiah Prophet Band: With metal music and searing songs, Messiah Prophet Band—sort of a junior Stryper—blasts out its message of salvation by "rocking the flock." Their music, says the group on one record sleeve, "grew out of the pure desire to reach out and offer the broken lives around us the power for living that the Father has given through His Son, Jesus Christ."

Geoff Moore: Though usually classified in the rock vein, Moore's music transcends labels and provides familiar ground for a variety of musical tastes from light to hard rock. While he says he is particularly concerned about young people, Moore sings powerfully about the frustrations and triumphs of the Christian life in a much broader context. He says the death of his father dramatically changed his life, strengthening and encouraging his faith and teaching a lesson he hopes to pass on, "that God moves in mysterious ways, troubling our hearts, yet soothing our spirits and giving us direction."

Rich Mullins: Mullins writes or co-writes almost all of his own music, music reminiscent of fifties rock with an eighties' flavor. When asked by *Gospel Music Today* about his ministry's goals, Mullins replied, "I think it's important for me to communicate that God is good—a good and loving God. Even though we will have problems in our lives, we don't need to be afraid of those problems. . . . When I write music I generally don't try to think of something to say. I try to understand what the music is saying, and I write the lyrics from that" (*Gospel Music Today*, 4–5/86, p. 31).

Michael James Murphy: Murphy began his career in contemporary Christian music, as guitarist for The Cruse, while still in high school. His solo career features music with a light pop feel and hookish lyrics. His concerts give a message of praise and commitment with an added dose of humor, as he draws from comedy imitations of Kermit the Frog and Elmer Fudd. "I love having fun at concerts," says Murphy. "I really stress the fact that God loves us to be joyful people. He came so that we would have abundant life, happiness and joy."

Larry Norman: "If I can encourage kids in facing their problems," says the blond, long-haired singer, "I'm happy." Norman makes it a high priority to meet and talk with his audience, bringing home the messages his music offers. "I tell them," says Norman, " 'Don't give up hope. You have nothing to worry about, our God is strong. Christ can solve all of our problems' " (*Cornerstone*, Vol. 14, Issue 75, p. 42).

Ben Okafor: Reggae music has steadily increased in popularity, and Nigerian-born Ben Okafor, now a Birmingham, England, resident, plans to "capitalize on that popularity to convey a Christian message to young people." The mainstream style of his music attracts openings into mainstream venues, and Okafor says Christian religious themes are easily integrated into reggae-style music because it originated as "the voice for the Rastafarian religion for many of those who perform it." His vision, he adds, is that his concerts should be evangelistic events to which Christians can enthusiastically invite their non-Christian friends.

Jamie Owens-Collins: Owens-Collins has completed numerous tours through England and Europe, New Zealand and the U.S., and is well-established as a singer and songwriter of contemporary Christian music appealing to all ages. Rather than just an opportunity to perform, she sees her music as a special way to "minister and share with others what God is doing in my life."

Her style, adds Owens-Collins, "isn't so radical that it turns older people off, but kids still enjoy it. And I think people respond to honesty. They know if you are putting them on—if you are just up doing your job because they paid to get in, or if you are really giving them something from your life. I really feel that my whole ministry is basically geared toward encouraging people."

Paradise: The press release from the publicity company— Schmaltz—said, "Feeling a little tired and listless? The strain of daily survival telling? . . . Well, don't despair." The solution, according to the release, is Paradise, a six-piece band who have become England's soul-rock lovers' favorites.

However, according to bassist Junior Edwards, the Christ-centered group suggests a better answer: "Our song is about our faith, our relationship with God, but we have to spell it out and we do so in interviews." Adds vocalist Paul Johnson, "We believe God is honoring our musical commitment. . . . He has given us a marvellous opportunity to witness" (*New Christian Media*, Vol. 3, Issue 4, p. 16).

Twila Paris: She comes from a missionary family and found a way to combine her own interest in missions with a love for music. Paris both sings and writes her mellow pop-rock Jesus music, striving, she says, to allow others to look inside her life and mind and discover what it is to be a Christian. Her lyrical message frequently centers on commitment, unity, and the individual's relationship with God. And, she adds, her vision for her ministry is ". . . to influence as many lives as possible for Him."

Leon Patillo: Leon Patillo hit the fast track to the top of mainstream rock music in 1973 as the lead singer and keyboard player for the secular group Santana. He left just as suddenly in 1977 for a whole new career with the same pop/rhythm and blues music, but a new set of goals. Patillo's gospel rock, however, is sometimes controversial, and his all-female, non-Christian backup band has caused quite a stir.

The singer feels hiring non-Christians is a way of evangelizing on a personal level. "I can truthfully say," he claims, "that this is almost like being back at a regular job and having to deal with people who are non-Christians and be an example. It's very challenging." Patillo also says he hired this particular lineup because it causes people to take notice—what he calls a "perfect setup": "As soon as they've got their mouths open or their hearts open and they're going 'Wow,' I'm gonna throw Jesus right down their throats" (*Contemporary Christian*, 10/85, p. 28).

Sandi Patti: Anyone even remotely interested in Christian music has heard of Sandi Patti. With sweet, classical sounds she has been encouraging the Body of Christ since 1981. "I used to feel that if I was not ministering to non-Christians, then I wasn't doing any good," she confesses. However, over the years, her vision has changed. "There is so much hurt among Christians," she now concludes, "so many decisions to make, and so much influence of the world, the church needs to be encouraged. . . . so what I am doing is encouraging my brothers and sisters in the faith" (*Charisma*, 2/86, p. 45).

Dan Peek: His decision to leave the secular folk-rock group, America, after recording eight gold albums, was Peek's first step in honoring a promise he'd made to God at age 19. "I remember praying to the Lord, 'If You will make me a success, I'll use that platform to spread the word about You.'" Within a year, his tune, "A Horse With No Name," was a number one hit.

That song's lyrics included drug references, but now Peek uses his notable songwriting abilities to talk about the Lord. "Maybe I can speak where others wouldn't be listened to. I want to write songs praising God for all He's done in my life," Peek reveals. "As a Christian, I am a tool to reach others. I'm like most other people; the things I've experienced can have meaning to someone else."

Petra: "Petra is edification, compassion, energy, music entertainment, ministry," says a spokesperson for the hard-rock band.

"Without a doubt, Petra is a blend of ministry and entertainment," asserts its founder Bob Hartman. "You'd have to say we are a delicate balance between the two. We don't apologize or make excuses to the fact that we entertain audiences. It is intentional, but we don't entertain at the expense of ministry. The ministry is bottom line. . . . What we have always wanted to be is an arm of the church, to where we can come into a city and work with the churches together, and see kids come to Christ and have the church [attendance] up as a result of the concert."

Philadelphia: With heavy metal music, and soaring vocals better understood by a teenager than his parent, this band has stirred up its share of controversy. When asked why they have taken this approach, Brian Clark, the band's bassist/vocalist, divulged the intent: "To reach the secular audience, the people who need to be reached for Jesus." Philadelphia hopes "Jesus is shown to be real and relevant, . . . reaching out with love" as their songs address such issues as child abuse, drug use, and the epidemic of runaways (*Contemporary Christian*, 4/86, p. 16).

Leslie Phillips: Creating something of substance, a Christian view of life that is not simply stereotypical fluff, is Leslie Phillips' goal. However, along with dealing with issues, she also sings songs of worship. She says, "I want everything to flow out of a sense of balance in my life. The praise songs I've written are really reflective of the way God has worked in my life, and I think He can use those little choruses to help people. And that side of me is just as important as dealing with some of the issues like premarital sex or suicide." Explains the pop-rocker with Cyndi Lauper/Pat Benatar vocals, "What I'm trying to communicate is that I want to be a balanced person, a whole person, in Jesus. I think that's what holiness is, really being whole and complete" (Chris Willman, *Contemporary Christian*, 1/86, p. 27).

Michele Pillar: When listening to Pillar, similarities with Carly

Simon and Linda Ronstadt are quite obvious. And she seems to appeal to the same type of fan as her secular counterparts, reaching out to them through her music, her testimony and her Christian single seminars. "I feel most at home with college-age people," she says, "because I was their age when the Lord taught me so much. When you've learned something at a certain spot in your life, you can minister to others at that spot because you know what they're thinking, what they're feeling, what they're going through" (*Christian Herald*, 6/85, p. 24).

The Predators: Their name and aggressive style were developed in their native England in 1980. According to lead guitarist Kelvin Allwood, they all feel they have been "called to the work." Lead singer Kevin Smith adds, "We like to provoke new thinking—challenge people with real and personal experiences . . . life and its problems. Surprise is on our side . . . because we appear at venues where no one expects to find a Christian band."

Prodigal: Loyd Boldman is the founder and key lyricist of Prodigal, a band singing in-depth lyrics to musical sounds varying from techno-rock to pop-jazz. Boldman volunteers, "We consider our work evangelism more than a ministry to the church, and we make a very concentrated effort not to clothe our songs in very 'churchy' types of things. We see the results of lots and lots of groups who claim they're evangelistic, but fill their songs full of paraphrased Scriptures or praise-the-Lord-alleluia stuff. . . . They're leaving unchurched people out in the cold because street people don't know what they're talking about.

"What we've tried to do," explains Boldman, "is to take it from a whole different tack and say, 'Look, here's something that is artistically engaging and has a certain amount of integrity as art, and has the power to grab somebody's mind as well as their heart, and make them think about themselves.' "

Quickflight: New wave synthesizers and eighties' rhythms dominate the music of Canada's Quickflight. The heart of the group is Ric DeGroot, who writes their listener-grabbing songs. "I have a strong desire to weld together 'new music' sounds with my own personal experiences and relationship with Christ," DeGroot offers, "and furthermore, to see this accepted as viable music by Christians and non-Christians alike."

Rez Band: Formed from within an evangelistic street ministry, Rez (formerly Resurrection Band) reflects its roots with gut-level rock and street-wise lyrics. While their methods have changed over the years (originally they played testimony-type folk music), Rez's over-all intention remains the same. "I think Rez Band needs to be a voice crying in the wilderness," enthuses Glenn Kaiser, the group's mainstay. "We're musical John the Baptists. . . . I think God's called us to be prophets. We're just a speck of sand on the beach, but I feel we do have a place to speak. . . . We get tired of Christian bands that just don't say anything lyrically." Kaiser laments, "Where are the prophets—the legitimate prophets? The world doesn't need more musicians. It needs real men and women of God who will deal with world problems and be real people."

Kaiser's wife Wendi echoes this vision. "We played in a hash bar in Amsterdam," she says, "and Glenn preached midst the glow of hash pipes. But we did a regular set and Glenn preached. If we can do that fine, but why would we want to play before more people, unless it was to preach the gospel?"

Kaiser has also said, however, the group lives in a Christian community where "change is the only constant." And while the band's lyrics remain characteristically bold, some of their methods have once again been modified. Their concert bookings and management are now handled by major secular music agencies, as they aim at a broader market. Halted are most altar calls and overt references to the Lord. Only time will tell whether this newest approach furthers or hinders their overall goal to be jamming Jeremiahs.

Cliff Richard: An unusual presence in rock and roll is India-born British rocker Cliff Richard. Believing that, because he is a Christian, nothing he ever does is "secular," Richard has hit mainstream as well as Christian rock music charts in England in legendary proportions, and performs on both stage and television. "I use my music," he once told *Circus* magazine. "My main motivation for being a rock singer is to propagate God's kingdom.

I want to prove in my lifetime that it's quite feasible to be both a rocker and a Christian, as I am. I just consider myself an entertainer who's Christian. I don't see why we have to split the two up" (4/30, 1981).

Cindy Richardson: A talented songwriter as well as vocalist, Richardson has had her songs recorded by Barbara Mandrell, Mac Davis, Sheena Easton and many other secular artists, and she was a backup vocalist with Crystal Gayle. However, in 1982, she reached a point in her life where she realized her need to renew a relationship with the Lord. "I was so miserable the night I came to the Lord," she confesses. "I had known Him as a child, and had strayed so far. . . . I wrote 'Save Me' that night and the song really says where I was and how I felt. All I want to do now is serve the Lord."

Rob Cassels Band: This band of dedicated Jesus music people plays gut-level eighties rock with a slightly southern flavor. Asserts leader and keyboardist Rob Cassels, "We feel constrained, whether it be proclamation evangelism from the stage or relational evangelism with the folk we meet along the way, to disciple and share the gospel with people, and this is the way we feel we can do it best" (Brian Quincy Newcomb, *Contemporary Christian,* 3/86, p. 12).

Connie Scott: Canadian-born techno-pop artist Connie Scott's desire is to be a musical missionary. "My goal is just being able to keep my heart open. To keep on giving 100% and be a strong Christian." She adds, "My goal is not to 'cross over' with my music," since every song talks about Jesus. It's not the kind of music, Scott explains, "where you say, 'Oh, this could be talking about a lover, or this song could be talking about the Lord.' . . . The Lord is the only reason I am doing this; He's the only person I want to talk about."

Servant: "We at least want to accomplish three things," states Owen Brock of the Cincinnati-based synth-rock, laser-light band Servant. "One is that we want to provide music that's an alternative for Christian kids—music they can identify with, that is Scripturally-based. The second thing is it's an opportunity for

Christians to evangelize their friends—people they have been sharing Christ with either at work or school. And the third thing we want to do is to challenge Christians in their commitment, in their relationship to Jesus Christ—that they consider the possibility of even going into full-time Christian work . . . and just to make sure that their relationship is really fresh."

77's: "We try to keep them from pelting us with tomatoes—that happened one time when the 77's sang a song about Jesus," offers 77's record producer Mary Neely, only half joking about the new wavers' goals. "But all of this is something we've been called to do—delivering the message," she's quick to add. "We want to penetrate the secular market, not for hits, or for recognition. We want to influence minds. And to reach the unsaved kids you gotta go where they are and play the type sounds they want to hear."

Second Chapter of Acts: "We all have the same goal," enthuses Acts' Annie Herring, "to see people set free. We're concerned about young people—young Christians who aren't really living a life for the Lord. So we want to offer support and challenge to Christians."

However, the singer and songwriter has some personal goals for her light contemporary music too. "When I am singing on stage, I want to give hope to people. The Spirit of God is so specific with each person. Each song ministers very differently to each person, according to their need. One of the things the Lord has been teaching me is that's His job, not mine."

Silverwind: Abba sound-alike, Silverwind, is known for its sweet harmonies and a bouncy European sound. The group's main interest is to see lives changed, to reflect one's need "for a deep relationship with Christ" and to bring, as Patty Gramling says, "a sweet song to the Lord." The evangelism orientation of Silverwind is nowhere more evident than its missionary outreaches. Tours have taken the group to Uganda, Kenya, South Africa and Poland.

Michael W. Smith: A talented young keyboardist, vocalist and songwriter, Smith's ultimate vision—to present a wholesome role model—sets him apart from the secular pop singers and rock stars he sees as his competition. "I want to be there as an alternative," he states. "Hopefully, they will look at me and say, 'How can he have such a great time and be so straight?' I want to be there to tell them they can."

Besides providing a lifestyle example, Smith says he wants to persuade young people to consider how their actions affect their world. "My songs are not preachy—at all," he adds. "But I do hope they make you think and make you re-examine your life. I don't think I need to give answers to everything. . . . But if I can make them think long and hard . . . then I will have hit the jackpot" (Michael McCall, *Contemporary Christian*, 6/86, p. 19).

Billy Sprague: Employing a free-and-easy pop vocal style, Sprague demonstrates impressive versatility when he performs everything from energetic synth-pop, to tender acoustic ballads. Sprague says he has three goals in mind for his music, the first two applying to Christians. First, to encourage his listeners to develop a "tender heart"—one attuned to God's slightest promptings. The second, to provide "encouragement and joy." The third focus of his music, however, is evangelistic, especially focusing on involvement with teens through Campus Life, Youth For Christ, and Young Life.

Paul Smith: Smith is a former Imperials member who is cutting out a successful solo career as a Christian pop singer. His aim, however, is not necessarily success in the usual sense. "My ministry is based on simple faith," asserts Smith, citing Romans 10:17. ("Faith comes from hearing, and hearing by the Word of Christ"—NASB.) "I think so many times we complicate the Gospel to where people can't understand it. I try to make sure that my songs and the messages in the songs are direct and easy to understand."

Candi Staton: "It's more than a song," claims this contemporary pop and soul-singing artist's literature; "it's a ministry of love, commitment and revival to the Body . . . to humanity."

Staton and her husband, John Sussewell, have a particular burden for the black family, they told *Charisma* magazine, because they see mostly women and children come to Christ at their concerts. "We also feel a special mission among black people, as a husband and wife, to encourage black men to be spiritual heads of their families. We need more unity in the family. That's where the devil attacks these days" (Jan White, *Charisma*, 2/85, p. 52).

Christian Stephens: Quality keyboards and acoustic guitar are an added feature of this dedicated artist's ministry. His main offering is a clear proclamation of the Gospel "to a world that desperately needs to know his love." But he's not above having a good time. "We hope audiences have as much fun at our concerts as we do," says Stephens. "Even though we're very serious about ministry and our music, we try not to take ourselves too seriously. We really feel an important part of our witness is just being ourselves on stage" (*Christian Activities Calendar*, 11–12/85, p. 34).

Randy Stonehill: Known worldwide for his unique, sharp-edged pop-rock stylings, as well as for his honest, funny, even somewhat satirical tunes, Stonehill says he writes his songs for whoever will listen, avoiding any attempt to appeal to any one group.

"I just want my songs to stand up as art," says the veteran artist, "and I try to write from my heart. I really believe in encouraging the body of Christ with my songs. Christians are my family, God's hands at work in this world. So I want to do whatever I can to encourage them."

Noting he also writes with an evangelistic bent, Stonehill adds, "That's an area where humor and satire can really be utilized very powerfully. You can confront people with their hypocrisy, their sin, their need for Jesus, in a pretty direct way . . . without their feeling you are talking down to them."

Noel Paul Stookey and Bodyworks: "Most gospel groups are singing 'How Do I Love Thee,' " points out Noel Paul Stookey, who still teams up occasionally with Peter and Mary to record and perform as the famous trio Peter, Paul and Mary. Of his Christian band, Bodyworks, he says, "We're singing, 'Let Me Count the Ways.' It may sound like subtle distinction, but for this band, it means everything."

In a similar style and with the same frankness, as his former folk-rock group, Stookey and his band serve up unconventional ideas for their listeners to ponder. "We're not evangelical in the traditional sense," he adds. "We may be a bit challenging, but the bottom line in our lives as well as in our music is our love for Christ and His love for us."

Stryper: Probably the most controversial Christian rock band, Stryper is up front with its testimony. Michael Sweet, the group's lead vocalist and guitarist, makes it clear that Stryper performs "more of a mainstream type music with a Christian message.

"We try to stay away from a title like 'contemporary Christian music' because we really don't seem to be that," Sweet says. The band's members realize they can provide alternatives for Christian teens who enjoy the heavy metal style of music, but that is not their goal. "We know what we want to do, what our goal is," he explains. "We want to reach people for Jesus. But we find that when people classify us as contemporary Christian artists, it actually takes away from what we're trying to achieve.

"We're trying to attract non-Christian audiences. We want kids who are into AC/DC or Mötley Crüe to be able to proudly say, 'Look, maybe I'm not a Christian yet, but I'm going to see Stryper.' Christians have to understand there are a lot of kids out there who need to be reached who aren't going to be reached by the way they do it. And—I'm being honest, if I wasn't being myself, I'd be a liar—I'm following what I think the Lord is telling me to do."

Donna Summer: The singer who made sexy disco an international phenomenon, Summer now talks of love's true meaning, as found in 1 Corinthians 13. In 1980 Summer abandoned an immoral, drug-filled lifestyle. However, she still chooses to record mainstream music, trusting that her new LP's present a different image.

Her producer, Michael Omartian, who is also a Christian, says Summer's new work is "a real assault on the kingdom of darkness—because Donna had always been associated with lust and various sensual pleasures. Now she has given all that up to really promote positive stuff." Her new message, says Omartian, isn't "blatant, but it feels so good that it opens the door to people being open about the Lord" (*Christian Contemporary,* 7/1983, p. 34).

Russ Taff: With a glossy, bluesy, barreling voice, Taff is making eighties music with a timeless message. The former Imperials singer says his break from the gospel quartet gave him an opportunity to travel abroad and expand his vision. "It did something to me to get out of our little 'Christian' environment," he told writer Bob Darden. "It made me realize the world is ready for God. But at the same time . . . the traditional ways of reaching those people have been left far behind. You just can't go up to a stranger and give him 'The Four Spiritual Laws' anymore. You've got to go beyond that" (*Contemporary Christian,* 7/85, p. 20).

John Michael Talbot: Talbot, younger brother to artist Terry Talbot, is probably one of the most recognizable figures in Christian music. His Gordon Lightfoot-like contemporary ballads offer much to the listener looking for quality worship music with messages that go beyond "milk" to the "meat" of the gospel.

"Because music has an inner spark that comes from the heart, it can also stir the heart of the listener," says the monk-turned-troubadour. "Music has incredible power. . . . Music symbolizes our love relationship with Jesus, and at the same time it makes that love burn stronger and brighter. The great Christian teacher Augustine said it long ago, 'He who sings prays twice' "(*Charisma,* 2/86, p. 22).

Terry Talbot: In 1973 Talbot was the leader of the country-rock band Mason Proffit, a group on the brink of superstar status. However, he left it all behind when he found Christ. "There's coming a time," he theorizes, "when many are going to realize how music can be used as a tremendous demonstration of God's power." With a genuine concern for commitment to Christ, Talbot plans to use the power. "I see the message of so much of gospel music being diluted today." However, with a heart for praise and evangelism, Talbot's goal is to bring "love and healing" to his listeners (*Christian Life,* 11/85, p. 45).

Steve Taylor: Wacky, witty, controversial and hard-hitting best describe Steve Taylor's music; however, he also strives to give his music a solid, biblical foundation.

He says his hyper-kinetic "new music" tunes have two main goals: "First, challenging young people to think about what it means to be a Christian in the 20th century—to develop a world view, to question authority and start using their own minds to get to a place where they are able to answer questions on their own instead of saying, 'Well, listen, I'll have to talk to someone else and then I'll get back to ya.' We all have to do that at certain times, but I'm afraid we're raising a generation of Biblical illiterates."

The wiry entertainer adds, "Secondly, I want to challenge those outside the Christian faith, because we do have a lot of people who are brought by friends to get saved. Our concerts attract people because they know they won't be preachy or insult their intelligence. We want to challenge those people that maybe they've gotten the wrong idea from TV or radio, but this is who Jesus really is."

Terms of Peace: Even though its songs rarely refer to Jesus directly, Terms of Peace—a band in the tradition of the Alarm—claim its music "ultimately points to Christ."

Guitarist Mark Case explains the artists don't plan to limit themselves to Christian audiences. Their goal, instead, is to "get out into the world and share Christ wherever we are . . . whether we're doing that backstage with other musicians, or with people we meet in the course of our everyday lives. We're not 'professional Christians'; we share our faith more off stage than on." Adds bassist Keith Moore, "The songs are a reflection of our everyday lives and experiences. . . . This is not simply a one-shot attempt at evangelism, but an effort to let the listeners get to know us as people."

B. J. Thomas: "I am a pop singer, okay?" B. J. Thomas told a European interviewer, clarifying his goals. "I sing for the populace, the masses. I don't sing for just one segment of people. . . . I record my music for everybody. I don't believe in organized religion. I think it's just a cop-out. . . . I'm not a fundamentalist Christian either, no. I mean, you know, I'm not a member of those born-again people—those Christians that are going to heaven while other people go to hell" (*Wittenburg Door*, Issue 80, p. 23).

Kathy Troccoli: Troccoli's reputation as a pop-jazz nightclub singer was growing steadily when, in 1978, she made her commitment to follow Christ. As a new Christian, she became devoted to "using the voice God had given me for Him" and she began to write songs about the things she was experiencing. Eventually, the deep-voiced singer came to Nashville to pursue a career as a Christian artist.

Explaining her motives, Troccoli says, "I try to relate to the audience in a way that any person out there can go, 'I've been where she's been,' or 'She's where I am.' I just want to encourage. And of course, I want to lead people to Christ. . . . I want them to hear a song in a way that will break their hearts so they'll be vulnerable enough to listen to the gospel message. And even with Christians, I want to take them out of the staleness, and let them know there is an abundant life out there."

Twenty Twenty: According to their literature, "Total commitment to Christ is the message of Twenty Twenty, whose musical talent and keen vision into the needs of today's young people puts them in an extraordinary position to change young lives." Ron Collins, lead vocalist for the Louisiana-based group influenced musically by the super-rock group Kansas, reveals, "I've always wanted to sing Christian music. I've never really wanted to sing anything else" (*Contemporary Christian*, 11/85, p. 25).

U2: A controversial band which has not hesitated to talk about touchy morality issues and politics, U2 pursues mainstream music. Not every member of this distinctive-sounding band is Christian, and their lyrics are purposefully un-preachy. They do not want, they say, to get labelled a Christian band. Lead singer and lyricist, Bono Vox, reveals, "You see, as a band we want to come off as a fresh, new thing. We want to offer hope, but we don't want to freak people out. We feel the Spirit is doing something different. Like Jesus taught in parables, and some of our lyrics are like that. Right now, we feel the world is trying to put us in a box and write us off as just another Christian band, and we don't want to be stereotyped like that" (Chris Ramsey, Keith Rintala, *Cornerstone*, Vol. 12, Issue 66, p. 40).

Very private about their faith, the members want their music to do the talking. Maintains guitarist Dave "The Edge" Evans, "People try to examine our beliefs to get a line on our music. But going the other way around is better. Music is a far better medium to explain something as personal and intangible as that" (Eric Levin, *People*, 2/11/85, p. 49). Another time he emphasized, "Don't ask me about my spirituality. Let's see whether my beliefs work. If they do, then they're relevant. If they don't, then forget it" (*U.S. Rock*, No. 58).

Undercover: Punk looks and ragged-rock sounds, coupled with an intense witness that is anything but "undercover," this Calvary Chapel-based California group is consistent—it never minces words. O-Joe Taylor, the group's keyboardist, says, "Our desire is to be credible to these kids, who, even though they are not violent, rebellious, satanic, punk rockers, they enjoy this style of music. We can reach them that way. But we also feel led to call, reach out to those people who are extremely violent. Now you can play any kind of music and be bold for the Lord. We don't have to justify playing loud and fast. The content of our music is the gospel of Jesus Christ" (Steven Vaughan, *Cornerstone*, Vol. 13, Issue 70, p. 37).

Concerning their bold, straight-on approach to music, Taylor points to the example of the apostles who "went out and witnessed hard core. . . . I'm not afraid to use His name, because it's a real part of my life. . . . We're taking Christ and His application to real problems in our lives and sharing those with other people: 'Man the power of God has changed me and it can change you too!' "

Vector: "Most Christian artists write to the Christian listener. But we're reaching out to others through our music," says Mary Neely, who represents Vector. Quickly becoming a favorite, especially with college-age young adults, this powerful, Rush sound-alike band has also made inroads into MTV's select few, where it can reach its goal of being a "positive force" as opposed to being solely an evangelistic group.

"The bottom line," relates chief lyricist for the group, Steve Griffith, "is that you establish a relationship and a trust between you and the person you're trying to talk to. You need to let them know you feel and think the same way they do, you go through the same things they go through—we all go through—every day. . . . I'd like to help whomever I can along the way . . . [and] let my songs and my life just speak for themselves" (Jon Trott, *Cornerstone*, Vol. 14, Issue 76, pp. 37, 44).

Reggie Vinson: Songwriter and musical performer Reggie Vinson has worked with mainstream megastars such as John Lennon, Alice Cooper, Kiss and Chuck Berry. When he discovered dreams-come-true aren't always fulfilling, he sought out lasting joy and found the Lord. Today, Vinson proclaims of rock music, "If it isn't saying the Word, there's no purpose for it. . . . In gospel music, if you're not saying the Word, you're missing out on the whole purpose of what God is doing.

"It doesn't matter now whether I get a gold record or not," adds Vinson. "A gold record to me is when I can tell some young person about Jesus and they get saved" (Kenneth Hagin Ministries, *Word of Faith*, pp. 6–7).

Vision: "Obviously, our goal is to win the lost," asserts Rocco Marshall, Vision's guitarist and lead vocalist. "The purpose of the band is to exalt the Lord Jesus Christ and take His message to a lost and dying world."

Says the southern rock group's spokesman, "We try to go out there and do our best and let God do the rest. Not just our best, but whatever it takes. We want to do something for Jesus that perhaps hasn't been done before, and so we try to just make ourselves faithful, available and teachable—mostly available. He'll use the person who's available more than anyone else, if you just say, 'Here I am, use me.' "

Sheila Walsh: Her literature says, "Music is meant to light candles in the darkness. Without that it has no meaning at all."

"The biggest thing I'd like to do," adds the Scottish-born pop singer, "is communicate to people who are not Christian, who have rejected Christianity 'cause they think it's not for them, and who actually have misconceptions of who God is. . . . The Lord knows my heart, He knows my real desire to get across to people who don't know Him. So I believe He opened that door."

Walsh also wants to dispel some mistaken notions about being a Christian: "There is a kind of image in Great Britain," she goes on, "that religion is a serious thing, a sober thing. These people [who come to my concerts] say, 'We didn't know it could be so much fun to be a Christian.' "

James Ward: No newcomer to Christian music, Ward offers up a smorgasbord of styles—jazz, pop, even black gospel—as well as a blend of motives. "A number of artists believe that music is only a tool to accomplish something else," Ward notes. "I believe that music is a legitimate task in itself; that art needs no justification."

That is not to say his music doesn't say anything worthwhile. On the contrary, most of his work is politically or socially oriented. "A lot of what I write is written for the church and the group of community believers," he says. "The Gospel has social implications, it calls all of us to action. It doesn't deny personal accountability. . . . It is important for Christian artists to be thinking people, and be identified with thoughtful causes instead of just rabid soul winning to the exclusion of all else" (Bob Darden, *Billboard*, 4/26/86).

Wayne Watson: Vocalist, songwriter, producer, musician—Watson is a man of many talents. In a style which reminds the listener of Dan Fogelberg, Watson communicates the gospel with sincerity. "I'm definitely trying to minister to the body of Christ," Watson discloses, "To point out things as I see them in myself and bring people to a realization of Christ in their homes, problems, and special circumstances."

Watson contends, "I think people will see me through the lyrics and music, and they'll feel free to say, 'I don't have to put on a fake smile just because I'm a Christian,' and 'It's okay to feel pain and grief and have my heart broken.' Jesus hurt! I think too many of us want to know Him in the power of His resurrection, but we don't want to walk with Him in the fellowship of His suffering. I think God wants us to know both."

Weber and the Buzztones: Keyboard-centered, wave music, with character singing that brings to mind a male version of Cyndi Lauper—that's the unique sound of Weber and the Buzztones. The California-based band has an equally unique outlook on Christian music's purpose: "In Southern California," explains founder and vocalist Larry Weber, "kids really want the bands to be 'cool.' We're not into the cool trip. We try to stay away from the image thing. If the Buzztones disappeared off the face of the earth tomorrow, it wouldn't be that great a loss. We're not a necessity. We're really not that important. We do have a message—we do have something to say. The message is, let's bring the families together and that's what's going to bring America together. But, I'm not some kind of awesome rock god. I'm a family man up there playing a guitar. That's the thing that I really try to show."

WhiteHeart: Since their debut in 1983, WhiteHeart has worked hard, lyrically as well as stylistically, to deserve its self-proclaimed title "Band of the Eighties." Though its style might well appeal to Duranies, the band enjoys wide appeal—Christian and non-Christian, 14 to 40. Lyricist and lead vocalist, Mark Gersmehl capsulates WhiteHeart's philosophy with one of the songs, "We Are His Hands, We Are His Feet."

"We want to magnify Jesus," he explains. "I know that's overly simplified, but I think I can speak for everybody in the group that the reason we do what we do is to let people know there's hope—that the Lord is the answer and He's the reason why we're doing what we're doing."

Adds guitarist Gordon Kennedy, "We are just putting the Lord's message to our music and trying to provide a serious alternative to young people. . . . We're just hopefully giving some good answers to a lot of questions they have, and doing it in a way everybody enjoys."

Deniece Williams: The girl who sings "Let's Hear It for the Boy" also wants to tell the world about the Lord, with her soulful blend of pop and dance music styles. Since establishing a personal relationship with Christ in 1981, Williams has been increasingly vocal about her spiritual beliefs. "We've come to realize," says Williams, "that this [music] is an excellent platform from which to speak about the love of Christ and what He is doing in our lives." That is why she includes at least one spiritual song on each of her LP's and performs only gospel songs for her concert encores.

Williams also works with Philip Bailey in a ministry she formed called the Living Epistles. "We do gospel shows and talk about being an entertainer who is Christian and how it is to try to live that kind of life" (Sandy Stert Benjamin, *Contemporary Christian*, 9/84, p. 19).

Mark Woodley: Mark Woodley is a Canadian singer and songwriter who ministers and sings about the concerns of today's youth, especially those alienated from the church. Whether in solo performances on acoustic piano and guitar, or with the rocking sounds of his band, Help, Woodley brings hope.

"Young people need to know that God is on their side," he says. "There's a lot of misrepresentation of the gospel. God has invited the whole world to receive His love and friendship. It's surprising how few know the simple truth of John 3:16" (*Gospel Music Today*, 4–5/86, p. 17).

Youth Choir: Sandy-haired, fresh-faced Derald Daugherty looks as if he just took off his choir robe when he bounces onstage. But when the band strikes its first chord, the image quickly changes to one of the The Edge or U2. "The music is basically a cultural thing," claims the guitarist/vocalist. "And God can use anything. We have chosen this kind of music as a vehicle for God."

With eighties' style music this band speaks to the decade's issues: abortion, hunger, youth suicide. Yet, the group says it respects the power of music, and tries to use it wisely. Explains Daugherty, "When you are up there on stage, people think of you as the voice of God or something—the same thing as a minister. It's dangerous to think you're God's voice, and yet you're only saying what you think. You have to be real careful."

Zero Option: England's Ralph Ward says that Zero Option is what you have when making a decision about God. "Above all," says the synthesized-punk rocker, "I want to give Christianity street appeal. I want to reach the kids who have never heard of Jesus, as well as those who may have become disillusioned with the idea of Christianity."

Personal vs. Universal Truths

Romans 14:5 says, "Let every one be fully convinced in his own mind" (RSV). If, after reading about the goals of some Christian rock groups, you are not convinced that the group's intentions are Spirit-led, or that they coincide with your needs or with where God has placed you right now—then it's important that you do *not* listen to that music until such time as God might direct you otherwise.

However, also remember that God is a personal God, and we are persons—individuals. God does not deal with us *enmasse* but one-on-one. We must do the same, not infringing on the freedom of others in areas that aren't moral issues. As music critic and pastor Jim Krupa says, "There is a tendency for many Christians to think that just because something is wrong for them, then it must be wrong for everybody."

On the contrary, the main point Paul makes in Romans 14, Krupa points out, is that a believer must make "personal decisions in certain areas as to whether or not certain items are sinful in his own life, and it is absolutely wrong for him to make his decision a universal principle for everybody in the church."

Let's be sure to use this information properly, to make personal, not universal, choices.

Chapter Nine

Graphics

If we are to judge at all, the fruit rather than the outward appearance clearly must be the basis.

—*John W. Styll, Editor,* Contemporary Christian Music

When we wrote *Why Knock Rock?*, it was much easier to discuss the subject of graphics. With scores of LP covers and video descriptions, we demonstrated mainstream rock music both knows and shows what it is all about. In both appearance and aspirations, many of secular rock's performers and promoters have declared it mainly is about—as punk manager Malcolm McClaren says—"sex, subversion and style."

However, the fruit of the music is the most telling, and the fruit resembles the music itself: many secular record shops look like porn shops, but with drug paraphernalia thrown in as a "convenience item"; punk fans wearing pins through their cheeks buy albums portraying punk rockers wearing pins through their cheeks; rock videos promote sex and violence as bedfellows, satanism as cool, and drug use as a road to the good life.

We are convinced Christian rock is worlds apart. However, a popular evangelist (and others) disagrees, claiming all Christian rock looks just like its secular counterpart. "I walk into a Christian bookstore, look over the record jackets, and think I'm back on Times Square in a punk rock music center," he protests indignantly. "Have you seen those covers lately? They are poor copies of wild, secular garbage. . . . The so-called Christian rock groups look like freaks, with demonic and witch-like expressions. They put serpents and other grotesque creatures on their [record] jackets. They are reflections out of hell itself. . . . Not only is the false god Baal behind it, not only is it demonic; much of it, I believe, has been conjured in homosexual minds under the influence of cocaine and other drugs."

And so while the world wallows in what *MusicLine* and *Contemporary Christian Music* magazine editor John Styll calls the "Prince/Madonna/satanic mudhole," the writer above would have us believe Christian rockers have created their own cesspool.

Though there have, no doubt, been excesses in contemporary music graphics, we have not found a Christian rock music album cover we would describe as drug-inspired, satanic or demonic. We do not deny that perhaps some may exist, but in our research we haven't found them. To give the impression that whole storefulls of such albums exist is sensationalistic and misleading—to say the least.

Even controversial covers such as Philadelphia's *Search and Destroy* album, with its dragon-skeletal demon figure; Predators' *Social Decay* sleeve, with its bony hand; or Degarmo and Key's conceptualized "666" video, which includes powerful shots of people turning into skeletons, faces melting into skulls, and a person representing the anti-Christ engulfed in flames, should not be viewed as satanic. Satan is depicted in the cover art or the video visuals because he is part of the subject matter of the music, but he certainly is not glorified. Describing these graphics satanic is as ludicrous as calling the Bible satanic because it includes accounts of demonic possession.

Prodigal is one of many bands who, because of contemporary-looking graphics, have been accused of satanic ties. Prodigal's leader, Loyd Boldman, offers, "In one of the 'Letters to the Editors' sections of *Contemporary Christian* magazine, someone wrote a letter saying our cover was satanic. The justification for his complaint was, 'When I look at a picture of Amy Grant's *Age to Age*—that's edifying.' Well, that cover is a picture of her, which raised the question in my mind, 'Why is a picture of Amy Grant edifying?' . . . a lot of it is simply in the eye of the beholder."

It's our conviction that the person who sees Baal-worship behind every contemporary Christian LP cover or concept video is confusing modern packaging techniques with worldliness or sin. "New" and "sin" may both be three-letter words, but that is about all they have in common.

Author Calvin Miller explains why Christians sometimes tend to be skeptical about anything "newfangled": "Generally speaking, we celebrate 'yesterday.' We revere the past, because Jesus worked there, but we're afraid of contemporary miracles, afraid God can't do anything in the present. We are sometimes so critical of anything new that the arts almost have to succeed without us, and then once they become successful, gradually we endorse them."

Boldman, who has studied art as well as music, concurs: "The joke is, if you want something to be okay in Christian circles, just wait ten years, and suddenly it's okay because it's no longer new. To me that's really kind of sad and shows how out of touch the average Christian is with what's really happening in the world around him."

Could it be that the One who "makes all things new" (Rev. 21:5) is also interested in new music? We think so, and yet, many Christians discriminate against the new and unfamiliar. It's a sort of reverse snobbism which sometimes allows mediocrity under the guise of spirituality, while superficially rejecting even the best contemporary artistic works.

Looking for Grandmas' Hearts

Jesus dealt with many equally controversial issues when He lived among us, and He often used parables as a simple but effective way to uncover faulty thinking. Were Jesus here today, He might use the story of Little Red Riding Hood to convince us to look deeper than the surface similarities between Christian and secular rock, and not to judge by appearances. For when Little Red Riding Hood went on her ill-fated visit, she found whom she surmised to be Grandmother waiting in Grandmother's bed, dressed in Grandmother's night clothes. Had Miss Hood judged the scene based on outward appearances, she would soon have become wolf-food.

Fortunately, she looked beyond the obvious, asked questions, watched for results, and discerned "Grandma's" true identity.

Had Jesus told Miss Hood's tale, He would probably have ended with a moral similar to "Beware of false grandmas who dress in flannel nightgowns, but inwardly are ravenous wolves. You will know them by their fruits."

Jesus never judged by outward appearances. In fact, when Jesus warned the Pharisees and scribes (whom He described as "white-washed tombs") that not everyone who sounds or looks good will "enter the kingdom of heaven," He explained what God does look for: "He who does the will of My Father who is in heaven" (Matt. 7:21, RSV).

God is not concerned with uniform appearance. He watches for results. Likewise, He's not concerned with how unconventional we look. His search is for "Grandmas' hearts," even if they come in wolf bodies. Regarding the unlovely and unfamiliar, He says, "Man looks on the outward appearance, but the Lord looks on the heart" (1 Sam. 16:7, RSV).

God knows there are wolves wrapped in Grandmas' pajamas, just as there are nice, little ol' grannies with exteriors as rough and threatening-looking as wolves. And He says we can tell the one from the other by discerning the results of what they do.

Editor John Styll says we must do the same when it comes to contemporary music artists: looking beyond surface appearances and judging the fruit of their work. "Look and see if they are doing the will of the Father. Are their lives and activities bearing fruit for the kingdom? If we are to judge at all, the fruit rather than the outward appearance clearly must be the basis. . . . Many out there whom you wouldn't want to take home to meet Mom are doing mighty things for God."[1]

While we look at the graphics of the Christian rock scene—how it appears visually and why—we must view it within this framework Jesus gives us, always looking for the fruit. Hopefully it will give us all food for thought about general performance appearance, album art and video concepts, and help us become better "fruit inspectors."

---

[1] *Contemporary Christian* (6/86), p. 4.

The Many Masks of Music

Today's Christian rockers have raised eyebrows among many more-conservative church members who simply can't understand or relate to what they deem outlandish appearances. We can understand how perplexing this issue is to those unaccustomed to youth culture.

Outward appearances—especially clothes—can communicate what a person is all about; they can make a statement. For example, a three-piece pin-stripe blue suit says, "I am a serious, trustworthy person." That's why the business suit has almost become a uniform among bankers. Likewise, a dark blue uniform, badge and black leather boots say, "I am a reliable person with authority." However, both of these examples express the intended message only within certain cultural boundaries. The "establishment"—which included both the wealthy and those with authority—was considered neither trustworthy nor reliable to the Yippies or Black Panthers of the sixties. To those cultural groups, the business suit and policeman's uniform said many things, none of them pleasant and few repeatable!

In much the same way, the Christian entertainers' performing clothes are tools for communicating to potential fans what the singers are all about. Their attire is a theatrical prop, much like the masks worn in the ancient theaters of Greece and Japan. In those cultures, the masks communicated something of the nature of the dramatic character so that—before a word was spoken—the audience knew if the actor represented good or evil, friend or foe.

Similarly, Christian rock artists often choose forms of dress to communicate something of their musical style before a single note is performed. The Altar Boys' Mike Stand explains, "It's just fashion. It's just a look. We're musicians and music is very visual—especially with videos—so we have to look 'visual' too."

Bill Findlay, who plays heavy metal-edged hard rock for Daniel Band, also describes their band's customary stage attire as fashion, "We've got the spandex pants and the studs and I've got leather boots that come up to my knees, and chains criss-crossed. It's just part of the dress code for that particular style of music.

But as soon as the concert's over," he adds comically, "even before I go out to talk to people, the first thing I do is get back into my blue jeans, running shoes, shirt and nice jacket." When asked if he felt hypocritical for wearing different clothes on stage than off, Findlay replied he did not. The stage clothes were just a costume. Classical musicians wear white tie and tails. In classical ballet, it's tutus and tights. "For us," says Findlay, "it's spandex and leather."

While this "dress code" may not be mandatory, it's difficult to imagine Rez Band playing the club circuit dressed in choir robes (a "costume" donned by church choirs). Likewise, John Michael Talbot's worship music would seem odd performed by a studs- and leather-clothed singer. It could be done, but somehow it would seem out of place or out of character. And so, leather and chains provide the typical costume of the hard rocker; wacky stylishness comprises the uniform of the new waver; flashy-colored spandex usually speaks for heavy metal; and earrings and multi-colored spiked hair function as punk rock's traditional mask.

Though rock music fans understand the language of the artform—because it is part of their culture—problems often arise when unaccustomed adults try to "translate" what the clothes are saying. Just as it might be difficult for a 20th-century citizen to understand the messages portrayed in the masks of Japan's centuries-old theater, many adults suffer "culture shock" when they attempt to decipher the graphic messages given by today's musicians through their stage look, their album covers and their videos.

Consequently, we get letters from parents wondering how any band with orange hair and black leather clothing can possibly be "of the Lord when they look sinful." "How can they even be Christians," the writers ask us, "when their album covers look so much 'like the world'?"

As parents and pastors ourselves, we understand how easy it is to react this way. We also occasionally suffer a bit of culture shock by misreading the look of a particular group. We see an earring on a male singer, and we read "homosexual." We see leather arm bands and we read "sadomasochism." For example, when we first saw the album cover for Vision's self-named LP, we were perplexed. Why the macho stance, grim faces and eerie emphasis on eyes? we asked ourselves. To us, it looked rebellious and menacing. In our adult culture, that is how the look translates. Does the group mean to portray that image? Is that how teenagers envision the group? Or are we misreading because of our cultural orientation? So we asked Vision's Rocco Marshall.

"You know, when you get our whole band together," the former cocaine distributor answered, "every testimony is pretty heavy. And we've learned you don't play games with God. We've learned that we've been called to war. And we're soldiers, we aren't 'wimps.' We're not little sissies running around. That's why the album cover looks like it does, because we mean business with the devil. We're not here to play games with anybody. We made that album cover the way we did to catch the eyes of the secular world—because we have a powerful testimony."

Suddenly the cover made sense. Album cover art, as well as clothing, is meant to capture a visual image of the songs inside, and this cover was doing just that. We had simply misread the message. We were glad we had checked it out.

We've experienced similar situations with other trappings of the rock music culture. However, when misunderstanding occurs, we advise adults to do two things. First, ask the band what it is trying to convey with its look—what is its message? Second, ask your child what message he receives from the look. If either answer doesn't measure up to godly standards, discuss the situation and, if necessary, avoid that group.

Both you and your children will be more content if you check things out. While you still may decide not to keep an LP because its cover seems inappropriate to your children's age levels or understanding, or the music just doesn't appeal to your personal tastes, at least you will have made an informed choice, rather than having jumped to a conclusion.

"I think we have made a tremendous and age-old mistake," offers rock artist Rob Frazier, "of confusing our personal taste with what's right and wrong. God is much bigger than our petty little tastes. . . ."

Is Leather "of the Lord"?

Our research of Christian rock graphics has convinced us Frazier is right; many Christians are not judging "with right judgment" even though the Bible often reminds us not to judge by appearances. In 2 Samuel 6:16, David offended his wife, who saw him dancing, singing and rejoicing before the Lord as the ark was brought to Jerusalem. Apparently Michal was offended because David's worship looked too much like the pagan Canaanites' worship. She called him shameless and vulgar (which sounds like some letters we've received describing Christian artists!).

No matter how outlandish David might have looked, however, his heart motives were right before the Lord. He was using the same *cultural* style of dancing and singing as his pagan peers, but he was offering it righteously to the one true God. The style was not intrinsically evil, and his intentions for its use were proper. It was Michal, on the other hand, whom God punished. She was reprimanded because she had "despised him in her heart" (1 Chron. 15:29) and hastily judged God's beloved servant. How important it becomes, then, for each of us to check out artists' goals—through music magazines, at concerts and the like—when we see something that appears questionable.

The New Testament likewise records two cases where appearances are mentioned: One speaks of an apparent nonconformist; the other, of worldly dress. In both instances, Jesus showed little regard for appearances.

John the Baptist, a nonconformist, was noted for his unusual attire as well as his strange eating habits—he wore camel hair and ate locusts. However, Jesus apparently wasn't offended by his outlandishness. In fact, John's appearance wasn't even made an issue (Matt. 3:4).

By contrast, Jesus railed against the established men of His day—the socially acceptable Sadducees and Pharisees—for making a show of their religiosity by the length of the fringe they wore. Condemning them as a "brood of vipers," Jesus made clear that appearances meant nothing to Him (Matt. 23:5).

Who are we, then, to condemn a musical group simply because they appear strange to us or they don't fit our own "normal" mold? Why do we insist our personal manner of dress is more acceptable? Aren't we confusing nonconformity with sinfulness and respectability with righteousness, just as the people in the Scriptures did? Our cultural upbringing to the contrary, we must remember Jesus never established a dress code describing the "Christian look." He never said, "You will know they are Christians by their hairstyles"; or, "I know my own and mine know me—we all wear shirts and ties."

Sweeping generalities of worldliness or sinfulness, based on outward appearances rather than thoughtful discernment, not only do a disservice to many Christian rock artists, but also limit their ministry capabilities. "It's a real shame that the church doesn't get behind their own," Rocco Marshall protests, "because the world certainly gets behind *their* own. And there's a lot of kids who will never set foot in a church, that will come to a concert, hear the music, and we'll be able to preach to them. Although we do entertain, we're there to win people to Jesus."

Nevertheless, according to George Verwer, some people, who live in "little suburbia" where everyone they know wears a suit and tie and has the same hair cut, "blow their silly little circuits when they walk into a Christian rock concert where there's a guy who has on leather and metal and lots of 'dangling things.'

"But they don't have to agree with the look," the evangelist continues. "They must simply be careful not to condemn other believers, or not to equate the Christian artist with [secular] rock groups down the road. . . ."

As Verwer suggests, there is nothing inherently evil with the color black, with leather, with earrings, with spiked arm bands. In certain cultural settings they convey immoral meanings, but in rock music they are simply fashions suitable to certain music styles. Certainly, they may have been used as symbols for something evil by secular artists, but there is nothing inherently evil in them. The point is, when we lump all people with green hair or spiked arm bands into the same category, classifying them as worldly or sinful, we run the risk of not only reading the wrong messages, but also judging according to appearances, instead of looking at the heart.

Faulty Thinking

We often also hear from people concerned with the biblical warning against conformity to the world. One such letter said, "The hairstyles and make-up are no different from those of punk rockers who are lost in the depths of sin. . . . They identify with the kingdom of this world by what they wear."

But, when the apostle Paul cautions, "Do not be conformed to this world" (Rom. 12:2, RSV), he is talking about attitudes, not makeup and hairstyles. That's why he adds, "But be transformed by the renewal of your *mind*" (author's italics). In other words, don't think the way the world thinks, but change your thinking with godly thoughts.

We're often tempted to take the easy way out, looking for the appearance of religion or evil, rather than looking at the heart. But this line of reasoning is, quite simply, a logical fallacy. The following are examples of this faulty reasoning:

Example #1

Premise 1: Christians often wear crosses.
Premise 2: Madonna, Prince and Billy Idol often wear crosses.
Conclusion: Therefore, Madonna, Prince and Billy Idol are Christians.

Example #2

Premise 1: Most cocaine traffickers wear suits.
Premise 2: Dan and Steve Peters wear suits.
Conclusion: Therefore, Dan and Steve Peters are cocaine traffickers.

The above conclusions seem ridiculous. However, we employ the same faulty logic when we say:

Premise 1: Secular rock musicians, who often promote sin and rebellion, dress in a certain style.
Premise 2: Christian rock artists wear the same styles.
Conclusion: Therefore, Christian rock artists promote sin and rebellion.

Protesting this illogical thinking, Rick Cua demands to know,

"What is wrong with leather? What is wrong with a leather jacket? I don't care who wears it! I don't care if the devil wears it! I mean, it's cowhide! The cowboys wore it. I mean, back in the old days, what did they put on their backs—polyester? No, animal skins. And yet, we take this stuff and we look at the bad element wearing it and we say, 'A-ha!' We forget about the hundreds of thousands of people who for years and years have worn leather!

"I can see how you might think the chains and the other stuff are a little 'weird,' " he concedes, "but if I had chains from head to foot, there'd be nothing sinful about it. It would be a little heavy, it would be a little stupid. But I'd do it if it would draw those kids in! I'm called to do what I'm doing right now," the lanky rocker insists, "and it's a focused part of music. Along with that music goes a certain dress—not a certain lifestyle, because I'm living the Christian lifestyle. But there's a certain form of music, a certain way to play it, and a certain look to it.

"I'm just trying to reach out to those kids, and say, 'Hey, you don't have to sell your leather jacket or stop wearing your hair the way you want. What you have to do is to be drawn to Jesus and accept the Lord, and the Lord will tell you what to do and when to do it.' "

Don't misunderstand. We're not saying that every leather-jacketed Christian rocker is an angel in diguise, anymore than it's true that every Mohawked young man is the devil personified. We agree with Cua, though, that it's simplistic to judge a book by its cover. What is important is that the artist reflect the gospel of Christ in his life and work.

"The bottom line," concludes solo artist Rob Frazier, "is the lifestyle, the sincerity, the spirit behind the person who writes and who performs . . . and the fruit. Are people being edified? Are they being built up in the Lord? Are they being brought into the body of Christ, or are they being driven out of it?"

We also see misunderstandings arise in reference to 1 Thessalonians 5:22: "Abstain from all appearance of evil." Modern versions, however, translate this differently—e.g., "Avoid every kind of evil" (NIV). This seems consistent with the rest of Scripture, since Jesus was called "a glutton and a drunkard, a friend of tax collectors and sinners" (Luke 7:34). Apparently Jesus wasn't afraid of the "appearance" of evil when identifying with sinners. First Thessalonians 5:22, therefore, doesn't give us license to judge by appearances. Instead, it encourages us to become fruit inspectors. Let's put the verse in context: "Quench not the Spirit," begins verse 19. "Despise not prophesyings. Prove all things; hold fast that which is good. Abstain from all appearance of evil."

In other words, Paul first tells us not to stifle the work of the Holy Spirit or treat inspired messages with contempt. Instead of tossing out these valuable aids to faith, Paul says to test everything. Try it out. See if it seems right and true. If things check out okay, hold on to it. If, on the other hand, it might be some kind of evil, avoid it.

As it applies to contemporary Christian music, then, this scripture (paraphrased) says: Don't squelch what could be a work of the Holy Spirit. Therefore, rather than judging by appearances, test for fruit. If you see good fruit coming from it—in your life or the life of others—grab on to it! We need all the help we can get! If, for some reason, the result is not good, then get it out of your life. It's not right for you.

Of course, we're not referring to obvious areas of sin—such as participation in satanic worship or sexual permissiveness—but to so-called "gray" areas needing more discernment. A recent seminar-goer misunderstood. She wrote: "If you say that it is all right for Rez Band to look the way they look to get the Gospel out, can a Christian female go to the beach dressed in a . . . g-string to give out tracts and witness?"

If any group's stage presentation, videos or album covers are offensive or a stumbling block to you because of past associations—or whatever—by all means, avoid them. But this concerned writer had missed the point we attempted to make in our seminar. We would never condone sin—in whatever form—as a means of "fitting in" with sinful people. Using lewd sexual enticement to "sell" the gospel is no more right today than in the days of the temple prostitutes. What we encourage is identifying with elements of a culture, not imitating sinful lifestyles. And though they may sometimes appear strange to unaccustomed eyes, to our knowledge Rez Band has never performed wearing immodest costumes. So, comparing their ministry to wearing a g-string while witnessing is similar to saying, "A youth group hands out tracts in front of a porn shop, so I guess I can star in a porn flick as long as I witness to the cameramen." One activity reaches out to sinners, the other participates in the sin.

Mike Stand, of the Altar Boys, explains, "When Jesus was here, He identified with the street people of the time, with the 'low lifes.' He didn't walk around with a 3-piece business suit on. Jesus identified with a certain culture, with a certain type of people. It's the same with us. We're trying to identify with a certain culture too—with some of the punk, new wave and heavy metal people."

As Stand suggests, though Jesus could have come to earth in any manner, He chose to come as a humble servant. He knew the crowds would not relate well to a temple priest dressed in tasseled finery. So Jesus came down to the people's level, but He never participated in the sins of those to whom He ministered.

Walking the Fine Line

All controversy aside, it's important we remember the trite-but-true saying, "A picture is worth a thousand words." In other words, a song can be full of the most beautiful, God-given music, but if it is wrapped in an unacceptable visual wrapper, a great deal of its value is lost.

In the same way, today's Christian artists must be certain not to cross that sometimes fine line between culture and immorality. "There are a couple folks," comments Rez Band's Glenn Kaiser, "who overdo it in the make-up. Some people overdo it in clothing. We just don't do that. It's crossing a line. We have to watch modesty and morals. But if it's just different, that doesn't mean it's ungodly. It's just a style, a culture, a custom."

Finding that balance Kaiser speaks of is very difficult and subject to interpretation. Stryper—with spandex pants and long hair—often hears protests that the group has crossed that line. Likewise, Amy Grant's LP covers and videos, as well as her candid comments about them, have elicited cries that she's gone too far.

In an interview with *Rolling Stone*, Grant raised eyebrows and a storm of protests when she said, "I'm trying to look sexy to sell a record" (6/6/86, p. 10). That line was picked up and picked over by nearly every major Christian periodical, without giving a sister in Christ the benefit of a doubt. We think Amy's remark, though tongue-in-cheek, was made unwisely, and realize Amy has not fared well when facing secular media, but her managers have not allowed us to ask her directly what she meant by that comment. We do know, however, that few critics quoted the rest of her *Rolling Stone* statement, in which Amy offers some explanation: "But what is sexy? To me, it's never been taking my shirt off or having my tongue sticking out." Apparently, Amy meant something quite different than the "sexy" that usually comes to mind—that Webster defines, "intended to excite sexual desire; erotic."

Certainly, Amy's new "look" has included a great deal of physical expressiveness—though we are hard-pressed to find anything erotic in her present performance or image. This look, however, reflects the trend among women toward increased physical activity and greater awareness of their physical selves. Amy therefore seems to understand that "a Christian young woman in the eighties" is very aware of her sexuality, which— biblically speaking—includes not only her body, but her entire personality.

In that context, the four-letter word *sexy* acquires a different connotation: A healthy, Christian ideal of sexuality. In contrast to the perverted views promoted by secular artists such as Madonna and Prince, Grant apparently desires to portray for young people a wholesome image of a Christian young woman, one who has moral standards but isn't a gloomy prude.

"Kids need love sung about—godly love, human sexual love sung about in a righteous way," says Don Finto, Grant's Belmont Church pastor, explaining why Grant's statement did not offend him. "A promoter once told me he hoped Amy would become a sex symbol, and I thought, 'Oh, no!' Then he explained what he meant by 'sex symbol.' He said, 'Amy's not the kind of person you'd want a one-night stand with. She's the kind of person every guy wants to bring home to Mom.' Now if that's what he means by sex symbol," Finto insists, "if she can portray the kind of person that a fellow would not want just for a night, but for a life-time, then that's godly."

Despite a wardrobe switch from lace to a leopard-skin jacket, and a smooth, contemporary stage presentation, the fresh-faced singer hardly qualifies as a Madonna look- or act-alike. "There are singers who only want and choose to sing for the church," Grant explains, "there's also a group of us that says, 'I believe in Jesus, He's changed my life, and I want to be part of my culture.' "[2] While her new image may not mesh with every Christian's personal tastes, it remains to be seen if she harvests more fruit because of it.

When we discussed images and modesty with lead vocalist Michael Sweet of Stryper, he echoed both Kaiser's and Grant's convictions: "People often mix their own personal taste with what is sin. God in His Word always lays down what sin is. He's very specific. Nowhere in His Word does He outline what you are to look like to know the Lord.

"In no way do I want to be sexually explicit," he adds, "but all you've got to do is compare us with those [secular] rock bands of today. Does Stryper have the seat of their pants cut out [as David Lee Roth has done]? Is Stryper sticking something in their pants to draw attention [as nearly every metal band has done at one time or another]?

"I could go on and on, but it's not necessary. It's too bad people can't realize where God is at work, but you can't please all of the people. Even Jesus got accused of casting out demons by using Satan. . . . It's a difficult situation, but I am here for the lost sheep. I would rather go and get one lost sheep than please ninety-nine saved sheep."

Sweet does have a point: compared to other secular heavy metal groups, Stryper is very mild in appearance. Their stage presentation—when we viewed it—didn't employ the crowd-enticing, sexually-suggestive posturing of most secular heavy metal concerts. And their LP covers and videos, though brash, have no sexual connotations.

However, we did press them further on the modesty of their

---

[2]*Contemporary Christian* (9/85).

costumes. Could they be a "stumbling block" to some? "If Christians enjoy our ministry, we appreciate it," they answer frankly. "However, if it is a stumbling block to you as a Christian, please do not attend our concerts, as we are going after the lost. Paul did this in 1 Corinthians 9:22–23. He became like all things to all men." The group concedes, however, "We are presently working on our costumes, to have them made a little looser. . . . We don't want to 'stumble' anyone."

We don't want anyone to be tempted either. But that is exactly why it is so difficult to set standards in this area. After all, what constitutes modesty is much more of a cultural and personal decision than a biblical one. African women often wear little more than a skirt, while Arab women seldom uncover their faces in mixed company. Their views on modesty are literally worlds apart.

Furthermore, standards fluctuate. At one time in the U.S., the sight of a man not wearing a shirt would have created a scandal. To be shirtless was to be immodest, even though it is now a normal occurrence. Likewise, in the late fifties, when "Beatle cuts" first appeared, many adults were scandalized by the "long-hair" look. By comparison, the new wave of teenage cropped cuts, reminiscent of styles from the fifties, now bring about the same parent-child battles (in reverse) that the earlier craze produced!

In the same vein, ballet dancers have worn spandex pants for years. The costumes give freedom of movement and don't detract from the overall mood, and few are bothered at the sight of male dancers in these tight-fitting costumes. And yet, many adults are outraged when the same costume appears on a heavy metal guitarist.

Which is right? And who decides what is a biblical or cultural notion of modesty—or immodesty? There are no easy answers to these questions. However, most of the Christian artists we have spoken to see it as one of their top priorities to continually seek God in setting standards for their stage clothes.

Let's review what some artists have to say about setting godly standards for graphics:

♦ "I take care not to go to extremes with anything," offers

Angie Lewis. "As Christians, we need to be even more sensitive to being a witness. It's a vehicle where we have a lot of eyes on us. And any little thing can be blown out of proportion or misunderstood. We should be very sensitive to that."

◗ Loyd Boldman would apply strict standards to the music as well as the look: "I think it's way past the time when we ought to be imitating the world as far as how we do things. . . . A lot of people nowadays—especially Christians—wait until some new pop thing happens and everyone jumps on it. Suddenly there's half a dozen Amy Grants or Michael McDonalds or Kenny Loggins sound-alikes. It's pretty much the same thing with looks. Take heavy metal: All of a sudden Christian bands are finding out, 'Oh! Heavy metal for the Lord! Let's all go rip our shirts and wear chains!'

"If that's what the Lord has called you to do and you're sure of it, then I can't say anything against you. But the idea that we are just reacting off of the world—just trying to imitate it—I don't think that's where we should be with music, album covers, or whatever."

◗ "I think it's good for all of us to search ourselves: Are we doing what God wants us to do?" agrees Bill Findlay of Daniel Band. "Is God pleased, is God indifferent or doesn't God like it? We should ask, 'Would you rather I not look like this Lord? What is it you want for me?' "

◗ Melody Green would add a couple more questions to Findlay's list—especially if an artist is using a more radical style of dress and music. "There are certain test points we can use to check motives," she explains, "but most important is to check our heart attitude: Is there a willingness to do whatever God wants? If God called us to wear, instead, three piece suits, would we? Are we seeking to glorify Him? Are we truly being called in this direction, or is it a cop-out? We need to watch that we don't try to manipulate God's will to our will, or God's timing to our timing."

◗ Lastly, Christian performer Pete Carlson adds a touch of balance to the graphics issue. He concedes, "Knowing how much I can affect lives is very humbling. It's a big responsibility and it keeps you in line." However, Carlson also admits it's comforting to remember that, in the final analysis, God's in control and "the package is not important. . . . But it's still the truth inside."

"Junk food music," explains **David Meece,** "is like cheesecake. An occasional piece of cheesecake now and then probably won't hurt you, but it . . . won't make you healthy and you can't live off it."

"For too long," declares Rocco Marshall of **Vision,** "we've seen these little 'paisley print' Christians. . . . Instead, I want to see some men of God go out and do business with the devil. . . . We came to rock the devil's socks off, to rock him off his throne."

Former Wings drummer **Joe English** says of his band, "We share testimony, scripture, and most of all, we're open to let the Lord lead each concert. We try to let people know Christ is real."

"God has called us to be a light in a dark place," maintains **Stryper's** Robert Sweet, "and rock and roll is a dark place. But the light can shine brighter in a dark place."

Kenny Marks (with Teri DeSario and Wayne Watson) desires that God would take his music—the energy, the songs—and use them for good. "I want my music to cut through the sediment and the tough stuff kids are living under today."

"We don't always provide a solution in our songs," notes **Servant's** founder and rhythm guitarist, Owen Brock. "We feel we're functioning almost prophetically when we deal with issues and bring them to the forefront, and say, 'What do you think? Are you concerned?' "

"Without a doubt," assures **Petra** spokesman and founder, Bob Hartman, "Petra is a blend of ministry and entertainment. You'd have to say a delicate balance of the two."

Soloist **Kathy Troccoli** explains, "I try to relate to the audience in a way that any person out there can go, 'I've been where she's been,' or 'She's where I am.' I want them to hear a song in a way that will break their hearts so they'll be vulnerable enough to listen to the gospel message."

Wendi Kaiser, **Rez Band's** gravel-voiced, powerhouse vocalist, asserts, "We don't preach an easy gospel. There is no crown without the cross. Repentance is absolutely crucial to your Christian walk. Or else it's just a cheap gospel."

"It's tough being a teenager in the 80's," insists solo performer **Michael W. Smith**; "all the pressure for drugs and sex. It's tough, and I'm out there to tell them there's an alternative—to say, 'Hey, there's a way out. You don't have to give in.' "

Hard-rocker **Rick Cua** argues, "When I wear a leather jacket and dress up like a rock and roller, and put chains on my boots or follow any of the rock and roll fashion trends, all I'm doing is reaching out to those kids who have going through their minds, all night and day, rock and roll, rock and roll, rock and roll."

Mike Stand of the **Altar Boys** makes no apologies for Christian rock and roll. "We realized the only way we were going to reach high school and college kids is to play the kind of music they listen to," he explains. "You have to use the proper form of communication. You can't sing hymns to them and expect them to come running down the aisles. They're just not going to listen."

The first Christian rock group to receive a Grammy nomination, and the first to receive MTV airplay, with their controversial video, *Six, Six, Six,* **Ed DeGarmo** and **Dana Key** strive to "communicate our faith and the Gospel to both believers and non-believers in the most contemporary music language available to us."

"I want people to know that I am just as human as they are," offers solo entertainer **Angie Lewis.** "I hurt just like they do. But I want them to know where I go, and where they need to go, to find the answers."

Of the demon/dragon figure glaring from the back album cover of the *Search and Destroy* LP, **Philadelphia's** Brian Clark says, "That's the typical 'metal' album cover these days. . . . But it's not just to imitate secular styles. First Peter 5:8 says, 'Your adversary, Satan, walks about as a roaring lion, seeking to devour.' Therefore the title *Search and Destroy* and that album cover."

O. Joe Taylor, **Undercover's** founder, admits, "On stage it's difficult sometimes to distinguish God's anointing from 'emotional rapture,' because music stirs emotions. Jesus said that it was His will we bear fruit—true—but also that our fruit should remain. So we look for a combination of those things."

"The joke is, if you want something to be okay in Christian circles," declares **Prodigal's** Loyd Boldman, "just wait ten years, and suddenly it's okay because it's no longer new. To me that's really kind of sad and shows how out of touch the average Christian is. . . ."

"My guitar's the same guitar as some other groups might use," points out Gordon Kennedy of **WhiteHeart**, "but my guitar is used as a weapon for a different kind of warfare. We're putting the Lord's message to our music and giving a lot of young kids a serious alternative."

"Everything I have to contribute is right there on stage," claims **Carman**. "The message is Jesus Christ, and I try to deliver it with as much universality and power as I can, because that's where He's at."

"I'll continue a dual career," clarifies **Philip Bailey** (shown with Leon Patillo), "doing Gospel as well as pop records while holding high the Christian standard. My music, whether secular or Gospel, no matter what I'm doing, I want them to see Jesus."

"After being a youth pastor for five years," explains **Steve Taylor** (pictured with Sheila Walsh), "I recognize that kids go through a certain stage where they have got to have heroes, and it's better for them to have heroes in Christian music than to have Twisted Sister or Ozzy Osbourne."

Sometimes, admits **Amy Grant**, "I ache because I just don't feel any closer to being who my heart really wants to be. . . . Then in a quiet moment, I remember that Jesus is somebody who always finishes the job He starts. . . . I start to feel that quiet unassuming peace filter back into my heart."

"A lot of my music is going to have a heavy message that isn't for everybody," **Debby Boone** stresses. "But along with it, I'm going to try and expand to a larger audience with things that I feel are important to everyone."

"I don't really separate my music and my walk with God," says **Steve Crumbacher**. "I want everything I do to be colored with Christ-likeness so that—no matter what I'm doing—others will know my main goal is to serve God."

Christian Rockers at the Crossroads

While God can conceivably use anything for good, Michael Sweet adds a very important point. Stryper, he maintains, has a specific goal: to reach the unsaved. That goal colors the group's entire look and sound. It also affects the type of fans it attracts. Given the members' intentions, a Stryper concert may be an inappropriate—even harmful—place to be for some Christians. Similarly, if Rez Band feels led to sing the club circuit, if DeGarmo and Key feel called to break into MTV's wasteland, if Grant wants to sing righteous love songs to primarily secular audiences, if Petra attempts a crossover into mainstream music, some Christians might find it necessary to no longer follow their music.

It's not advisable, for instance, for most young Christians to watch hours of MTV simply to catch Degarmo and Key's "666." Likewise, most Christians would do well to stay away from bars, even if Rez Band is appearing there.

That's why it is so important to keep current on artists' goals—because they change. Several years ago, Michael W. Smith was writing and recording praise songs for the church. Now he's attempting to cross over with a new style and new songs for the unsaved. His first goal was no better than his second, just different. However, a lifelong Christian looking for "meat" in his music may no longer find it in Smith's tunes if he serves mostly "milk" music for the unsaved or newly reborn.

When these changes come, let's not jealously hold tight to our Christian performers, never allowing them to develop. As writer Patrick Kampert says, "When you lose your ability to change, at that moment, you begin to lose your relevance."[3] It's important that we allow Christian artists the flexibility to test new avenues.

We have experienced the same need for growing room in our ministry. Only a few years ago, we were pastors of a young, vibrant church in North St. Paul, Minn. However, a quickly planned rock music seminar and a subsequent record-burning media event changed all that. Within a short time we needed to

---

[3]Patrick Kampert, "Roots of the Contemporary Sound," *Christian Life* (11/85), p. 51.

make some changes, going full time with Truth About Rock, but remaining under the godly authority at Zion Christian Center. When we did, our congregation gave us their blessing.

Had they not prayerfully released us to our new ministry, literally hundreds of thousands of teens would not have heard about the dangers of rock and roll—but more importantly, young people throughout the nation would not have been introduced to the saving power of Jesus. In the same way, we sometimes need to "let go" of artists at the crossroads of new ministries.

Let's not allow our pettiness, undue criticism, or envy to keep Christian artists from growing and changing as they try to listen to God's personal call. And in all humility, let's also give them the freedom to experiment and to make mistakes. Let's give them support and encouragement, and—if we don't approve of changes they make—let's pray for them rather than attack them.

Movement across cultural barriers has always brought a degree of suspicion, misunderstanding and uncertainty. But if we remember to look for Grandmas' hearts, even if they are enveloped in wolves' bodies, we'll learn how to best fight the excesses and forgive the errors as Christian rock music strives for new goals.

Part Three

Concerts and Questions

You bring in kids when you appeal first of all to their senses—hearing and seeing. When you have their attention, then you can preach to them.

—Rocco Marshall, Vision

"Entertainment plays an important part in the life of a child," observes New York University's theater program director, Nellie McCaslin. "To the extent that it is selected with judgment and care, entertainment contributes to his or her social, intellectual, and emotional development."[1]

The entertainment young people experience is an integral part of the growth process, and as a caring parent, you want to help them learn to choose their musical entertainment wisely. In the next chapters we'll discuss one of the major entertainment resources available to Christian young people—the Christian

---

[1]From the foreword to Muriel Broadman, *Understanding Your Child's Entertainment* (New York: Harper & Row, 1977), p. vii.

concert. Then, because we realize Christian rock music poses some prickly issues, we'll field your most common questions and challenges on the subject. Finally, in a spirit of care and concern, we offer a heartfelt open letter to artists who might read this book.

Chapter Ten

The Concert: Rock Music's Mainstay

What is the "spiritual" look? . . . If these people feel they want to dress in a dramatic way to reach a particular audience, in order to break down this idea that Christians are all the same, then may the Lord use them!

—George Verwer, International Director of Operation Mobilization

In the secular concert scene, it seems the more bizarre the better. And while heavy metal bands evoke the most rebellion and violence at concerts, even the mildest mainstream groups attract unseemly behavior. Robberies, rapes, car thefts, stabbings, gang fights, rioting—all occur with frequency.

A report from Community Families in Action says, "At rock concerts, sometimes youngsters are exposed to alcohol and drugs, pornography, profanity, cruelty, and in some instances, to life-threatening situations in large unruly crowds in concert halls." Law-enforcement officials agree, but say there is little they can do. "The louder the rock, the nastier the show," observes Fort Worth, Texas, Police Captain Ray Armand, following a Ted Nugent concert at which a bare-breasted fan was fondled on-stage by the star.[1]

Backstage, apparently, the scene is even worse. Reporter Brent Staples, of the *Chicago Sun-Times*, says one security guard he interviewed "has heard every conceivable scam and had offers

---

[1]Thomas Korosec, *Fort Worth Star-Telegram* (4/24/86), p. c1.

of 'every conceivable sexual favor' for a guarantee of safe transport into the bands' dressing rooms."[2]

What elicits such behavior from otherwise "good" teenagers? The bands, it seems, plan and promote it. Says Rolling Stones' Mick Jagger, "The only performance that really makes it is one that achieves madness." Likewise, when 145 people at a rock festival were arrested for incidents ranging from murder to drug possession, ex-Van Halenite, David Lee Roth, angered law-enforcement officials by inciting the crowd with comments such as, "More people have been arrested today alone than all weekend last year! You guys are a bunch of rowdy mother——!"[3]

Coming Through Loud and Clear

Enrapt by a secular concert's sights and sounds, a young fan of 14 or 15 years old is in a most suggestible mental state—open to the messages of the music—and those messages are loud and clear. Blatant odes to permissive sex and drug and alcohol use abound, as do obvious enticements to rebellion and violence.

At a Billy Squier concert the crowd responded with unrestrained enthusiasm when he directed their attention toward his crotch. According to *Rolling Stone*, "Knowing he was onto a good thing, Squier concluded one song with a blatant f— pantomime, grimly dry-humping the stage."[4]

In-concert antics of the LA-based Red Hot Chili Peppers have likewise caused concern. As part of their usual encore repertoire, says frontman Anthony Kiedis, the singers "get naked, take a sock and put it over our privates, then go out and do this song called, 'Stranded,' which is about being in the bathroom with no toilet paper."[5]

Prince, whose concerts were 1985's top box office success, featured simulated oral sex (by both himself and his opening act, Sheila E.), a phallic guitar that shot liquid after being caressed,

---

[2]Brent Staples, "Bartering with their bucks, bodies," *Chicago Sun-Times* (4/30/84), p. 29.
[3]"Violence Mars US Festival," *Rolling Stone* (7/7/83), p. 46.
[4]*Rolling Stone* (11/8/84), p. 56.
[5]*Star Hits* (4/85), p. 5.

and Prince bathing onstage—sometimes inviting a member of the audience to join him.

Wrathchild, from Worcestershire, England, features in its stage show naked women, whips and chains. "It's part of our overall presentation," says vocalist Rocky Shades. "We are trash. We play trash metal and we look like trash."[6]

Another brutish British power trio, Raven, features a helmeted drummer named Wacko and an incredible stage setup. "We're acting crazier than ever," says guitarist Mark Gallagher. "We've been cracking beer bottles over Wacko's head . . . and I've been smashing up so many guitars that the guitar roadies are going a bit crazy."[7]

Security guard Allan Fugate, of Louisville, Ky., says people at rock concerts all go a bit crazy. Marijuana smoke casts a blue haze, and nudity, lewd behavior and violence are commonplace. It's normal, he says, to confiscate 20 to 30 knives and guns from patrons entering an arena.

"Peer pressure is a big thing at rock concerts," Fugate says, "and if you get in an environment where there is no authority— and that's what a rock concert is, total absence of authority— you're going to see the worst behavior as a general rule."

What's the answer? According to Fugate, "The best thing would be not to be there. I would not let my kids go to a rock concert, because it's dangerous! You can get hurt there! I think a big thing would be education for the parents and education for the children. I'd like to see some of the parents go to a concert just once—the kids wouldn't be there the next time."

Some parents are beginning to get educated, and are taking action as well. In Savannah, Ga., a letter-writing campaign against Black Sabbath's appearance succeeded in getting the group's concert cancelled. And in San Antonio, Tex., a new ordinance bars unescorted children from rock concerts at a city arena if the performers depict certain sexual acts in their songs or stage behavior.

---

[6]*Hit Parader* (5/85), p. 42.
[7]*Hit Parader* (9/85), p. 56.

Communicating God's Love

We concur with this legislation of secular rock concert standards. In fact, we believe secular concerts are inappropriate for most teenagers, even when accompanied by adults and even if they promote acceptable rock groups. No matter which band performs, drugs, immorality and violence are almost always in evidence at secular concerts.

Instead, we advise teens to check out the contemporary Christian music scene. "There is a tremendous difference between our concerts and the rock concert," says Petra's Bob Hartman. "When we start singing our songs, we start expressing our faith in Jesus Christ as our Savior—and also in the exhortation between the songs. That's definitely different from the rock concerts!"

The dynamic Leslie Phillips also wants to put parents' minds at ease. "Just because I do Christian rock," she says, "that doesn't mean I eat nails for breakfast. Most people's conception of Christian rock is based on their ideas about non-Christian rock bands and performers, particularly the 'heavy metal' bunch. My music isn't like that at all. I'm into communicating God's love to young people in a way that they can understand."[8]

The secular press doesn't know quite what to think of Christian concerts, but the distinct difference is not lost on them. Says Don McLeese, of the *Chicago Sun-Times*: "Woodstock idealism aside, rock festivals are usually a mess. They're often marked by drug overdose, alcohol overindulgences and the sort of open nudity and rampant sexuality that one generally doesn't experience in polite society. . . . They seem to have lost their sense of purpose.

"At the Lake County Fairgrounds this weekend there's a [Christian] rock festival that is expected to be well-attended, well-behaved and full of purpose. . . . The musical styles may suggest Van Halen and Quiet Riot or Talking Heads and Elvis Costello, but the lyrics are predominantly about saving souls."[9]

---

[8]*Greenbelt '85 Programme*, p. 62.
[9]Don McLeese, "Rock," *Chicago Sun-Times* (6/20/84), p. 67.

"Praising God Lustily"

Unfortunately, some parents aren't quite certain what to think of Christian rock concerts either. We can certainly understand their concern—there are perhaps surface similarities. But one doesn't have to look too closely to see there are also major differences. At most Christian concerts, one sees artists and fans apparently taking seriously the advice of John Wesley, the founder of the Methodist church: "Sing, not lulling at ease or in the indolent posture of sitting, drawling out one word after another, but all standing before God, and praising Him lustily, and with good courage." Unfortunately, it's sometimes that same loud singing and exuberant praise, combined with often offbeat costuming, that causes some adults to wonder if the concert is a righteous place for their young people.

While it's important to use discernment in deciding which Christian concerts are appropriate for you or your teens, environmentally, most, are in our opinion, not only acceptable but helpful for young Christians and those they would like to evangelize.

Christian rock musicians may look like their secular counter-parts—right down to pink hair or black leather pants—and their concerts may include all the latest laser light technology, but they see themselves as evangelists who use music both to spread the gospel and challenge Christian kids. "We're primarily ministers," says O-Joe Taylor, spokesman for the Calvary Chapel-based band, Undercover, "and we use music only as a tool to bring people to Jesus."

Taylor and others like him believe their appearance—though irrelevant to their faith—provides an avenue into today's teenage culture. If I were dressed up in a suit," he insists, "I couldn't . . . expect kids who are into heavy metal or punk to listen to me." Taylor, who sports a modified mohawk, and wears chains and leather, says, "I don't think the outside is that important. God is concerned with the inward man."

George Verwer, International Director of Operation Mobilization, agrees: "What is the 'spiritual' look? Is it the Mormon look? When Mormons arrived in England, they looked like they had just come out of the First Baptist Church. They had their ties on, they had their white collars, they were usually blue-eyed Anglo-Saxons. Is that the 'spiritual' look?

"We have driven more people away from God and the Bible and Jesus Christ through making the narrow road twice as narrow. It has always been narrow—to believe the Bible is God's word, to believe in heaven, to believe in hell. . . . [But] if these people feel they want to dress in a dramatic way to reach a particular audience, in order to break down this idea that Christians are all the same, then may the Lord use them!"

Rick Cua is one Christian rock artist who is trying to break down that notion. He says, "There are a lot of kids out there who need the Lord real bad. And now, they can look at me—not just the church kids, but the secular community—and say, 'Hey, I know this guy from the Outlaws and he plays great music, and he's playing Christian rock? I don't even know what that is, but he looks like he used to and the music sounds great. I want to hear what he's got to say.'

"I'm called to do rock and roll—a very focused kind of rock and roll, and along with that goes a certain dress. Not a certain lifestyle—because I'm living a Christian lifestyle—but a certain art form, and there's a certain way to play it and a certain look to it."

Christian Cultural Lobotomy

Servant is another group whose members use today's concert format to appeal to today's youth. Their imaginative stage presentation and innovative light show have won them praise as one of the most professional-looking groups in Christian music. Owen Brock, the group's founder, says, "We feel we have two goals. One is to be an alternative to Christians, so that they can be edified. If they are used to listening to more upbeat music, and then they become Christians, they don't need to have a cultural lobotomy. We give them something they can identify with.

"The second goal is to provide a way Christians can evangelize their friends. If they have been sharing Christ with their friends at work or at school, we can help by coming in and supporting that. They can take their friends to a concert and they can say, 'Listen, these guys will relate to you right where you're at.' Even if they don't become a Christian from hearing our message— and we give an altar call at the end of each concert—at least their stereotypes about Christianity have been thrown out the window."

Another stereotype dispelled by the new breed of Christian concerts is that they are more subdued than the secular scene. Christian crowds have become as animated as the music. The sight of several thousand kids on their feet, clapping to the beat, might concern some parents. In fact, we have viewed concert commotion quite skeptically ourselves in the past. The excitement and emotion generated at Christian concerts, however, can be a positive thing. As J. Brent Bill, author of *Rock and Roll: Proceed with Caution* says, "If emotional involvement makes a song bad, where would that leave school fight songs? Or . . . hymns of the church? I admit rock and roll involves me. So does Beethoven."[10]

---

[10]J. Brent Bill, *Rock and Roll: Proceed with Caution* (Old Tappan, N.J.: Fleming H. Revell, 1984), p. 79.

As parents, we need to remember that these are more often matters of taste than of morality. After all, groups of musicians were employed even for Temple service in Israel during Bible times, and the Israelites certainly were not a reserved people. The Bible makes no apology for times when God's people joyfully danced and shouted to energetic rhythmic music. Pop music is upbeat by nature and when you add uplifting lyrics about the Lord, it's no wonder kids want to get up off their feet and start clapping their hands and moving. Regarding her more contemporary, invigorating music of late, Amy Grant says, "There's just times in the concert—if I were sitting in a seat, I just couldn't sit still."[11] We need to ask ourselves, is "sitting still" more Christian than not sitting still? As long as decency is maintained, what harm can come from a few hours of boisterous, beat-filled fun?

Christian entertainer Rob Frazier says, "A lot of times the young kids are just overwhelmed by the whole music package and they really look up to us artists. I just try to transform that energy they are giving us to the Lord."

At first glance, a group of bobbing kids at a Christian concert may look similar to secular concert-goers. It's important to note, however, that as veteran rock critic Bob Larson says, "There's a difference between erotic boy-meets-girl disco-fever and what goes on at contemporary Christian concerts."[12] Likewise, the drugs, violence and lewd behavior so prevalent at secular venues seldom surface in the Christian scene. Instead, there is a camaraderie and a wholesome joyfulness at most Christian concerts that is difficult to describe to one who has never experienced it.

Author Calvin Miller puts it this way: "The whole rock thing—in letting the music predominate—brings together a strong feeling of community at rock concerts that is often missing at more sedate kinds of things. . . . If the church were supplying close camaraderie that seems to weld whole auditoriums and arenas full of young people together, if we could just figure out how to bring about that same strong sense of community . . . we would have gone a long way toward interesting the world in Jesus Christ."

---

[11]*Minneapolis Star-Tribune* (4/18/86), p. 4C.
[12]*Contemporary Christian* (12/85), p. 7.

That's Entertainment

The word entertain has two meanings: to serve food to, or to amuse. Both meanings are applicable to Christian entertainment, which can feed and be fun. While entertainment is an effective tool in the work of modern ministry, there is nothing wrong with simply having a good time.

"So many people have the misconception that being a Christian means hiding in the closet," says entertainer Greg X. Volz, "and not having fun of any kind. But we have a tremendous time at our concerts. . . . It's a full-fledged rock 'n' roll show, but with a difference."[13]

Don Finto, pastor of Belmont Church where Amy Grant and her musician-husband Gary Chapman attend, says, "Every time I see one of their concerts I am grateful that, in this confusing generation, the Lord has opened doors for Amy, Gary and others to speak to the hearts of today's youth. They are playing to hundreds of thousands across the U.S., and their message is uncompromisingly clear. The medium is pop music and they are catching the ears of America."

As long as entertainers don't attempt to create a "fun" gospel there need not be a line drawn between hearing the Good News and having a good time. After all, Jesus even used an entertaining medium—parables—to "catch ears" and then teach the people of His time the principles of the Kingdom. In the same way, when Billy Graham pauses effectively or Jimmy Swaggert dramatically strides the stage, they too, are using elements of entertainment.

There is purpose in such technique, contends Christian performer Carman (Licciardello). It is, he says, a way of communicating. "When you communicate, you're seeking to captivate their attention. It's something you have to earn. No one can demand to be listened to. You've got to establish trust, a rapport. That's what communicating is all about. That's what entertaining means."[14]

---

[13]Linda Thornton, "Rock of ages isn't what it used to be," *Miami Herald* (3/1/85).
[14]Davin Seay, "Carman," *Contemporary Christian* (5/85), p. 22.

Not a Substitute for Worship

Still, we must remember to keep music and concert-going in proper perspective. If we need entertainment to draw us to God, something is wrong with our priorities. As A. W. Tozer once said, "It is scarcely possible in most places to get anyone to attend a meeting where the only attraction is God."[15] We need to ask ourselves if we entertain thoughts of God only when we find them entertaining, or if we seek to know God even when it's not so fun.

Likewise, a late Saturday night concert should never become an excuse for not attending services on Sunday morning. Jeff Crandall of the Altar Boys says we can have fun, be entertained, lifted and edified by concerts, but light shows and guitar licks should never be a substitute for worship. "It has come to my attention," he warns, "that this is happening today among a lot of the people that are into Christian music. But the Bible says we are to seek first God's kingdom and His righteousness (Matt. 6:33). God should be your first love. . . . It may mean putting away your albums for awhile, not going to concerts . . . but do whatever you need to do. . . . They just shouldn't be your reason for living. When someone asks you what you're into, don't say you're into the Altar Boys, Undercover, Stryper or Rez Band. Just say, 'I'm into God and God is into me.' "

Perhaps some parents would find it helpful to hear what other parents who have actually accompanied their teenagers to Christian concerts have to say:

"I was at the Rez concert . . . and no offense at all, but their music is not my favorite taste. . . . But to my surprise, as Wendi [Kaiser] started to speak the first time, the Spirit of the Lord fell on me in such power that I just started to cry! . . . I can't tell you what exactly happened, I only know I walked away changed and seeing more clearly another part of God's character and his ability to minister to his people through rock 'n' roll music!"

"After taking my daughter to [Amy Grant's] Atlanta stop of the *Unguarded* tour, I can only say, 'Thank you for the role model you provide for her.' "

---

[15] A.W. Tozer, "Man: The Dwelling Place of God."

"We went to Steve Camp's *Wake Me to Shake Me* tour concert. It was loud, especially when Rick Cua and Rob Frazier were playing, but when Camp shared with those kids about how the Lord was working in his life, he was real and his words were convicting. Within minutes, that auditorium went from noisiness and clapping to prayerful quiet, and I watched kids join hands in small groups and pray for one another."

"I loved Geoff Moore, and I *could* get used to these guys, but I'd turn the decibels down just a tad! I have a 15-year-old, a 19-year-old and a 20-year-old, and I think it's a wonderful place for them to be."

"There were a few numbers that were loud and 'rock and roll-y' but basically, it was all done in a good spirit. I stopped in to see what was going on and basically watched the crowd. . . . They were praising the Lord and having a good time."

"I guess the greatest evidence I have that Christian music is not harmful, is my children . . . They are rare in a world where Christians, young and old, compromise in many areas of their lives. . . . I attribute much of this to the influence of Christian music through the years."

Chapter Eleven

Playing Hide and Seek

We can't develop aesthetic standards and discrimination unless we are willing to be open-minded toward what is new and unfamiliar, even if we don't at first understand it.

—*Frank Gaebelein*

Hide and Seek is supposedly a children's game, yet, during our years of presenting Truth About Rock Seminars, we have often seen people of all ages playing a version of the game. These are people who may want to seek God's truth, but they also hide a desire to keep their secular rock music favorites. Consequently, they grill us with what we have affectionately termed "yeah-buts"—challenges to our claim that most secular rock music is harmful. Some of the yeah-buts we hear most often are, "Yeah-but, how can they hurt me when I never listen to the lyrics?"; "Yeah-but, who are you to say what's right or wrong?"; "Yeah-but, aren't you advocating censorship?" or "Yeah-but, why do you burn records?" (If you are still concealing some yeah-buts about secular rock music, our books *Why Knock Rock?* and *Rock's Hidden Persuader* will give you some solid answers.)

We were surprised, however, that when we began introducing our seminar-goers to secular rock alternatives—Christian contemporary music—we experienced some Christians playing a similar Hide and Seek Game. These people, also seekers of God's truth, hide their desire to hold tightly their notions about the style of rock music. Their yeah-buts may be different, but the game's the same. And while we've found teens more adept at version one, parents seem the pros at version two!

All of us find it more comfortable to protect our pet ideas

than grapple with the issues. As Frank Gaebelein argued, however, "We can't develop aesthetic standards and discrimination unless we are willing to be open-minded toward what is new and unfamiliar, even if we don't at first understand it."[1]

The following is a sampling of the most frequent challenges we receive to our position on Christian rock. We don't claim to have all the answers, but we hope our responses will help settle any yeah-buts you may have, or at least give you some ideas to think about.

I heard that a missionary had taken a former witch doctor to a Christian rock fest, and the witch doctor asked, "Why are they playing that music? That beat calls up demons!" How can this primitive voodoo beat, borrowed from African pagans, be used for Christian music?

We have heard this story in so many variations, we have lost count. One report said former TV talk show host Jack Paar, while on safari in Africa, witnessed natives "coming alive" when some American musicians began playing rock music! "This was their beat," the account explained.

We believe the devil—while not behind the beat—is behind these stories. As the hoax concerning Proctor and Gamble's logo, or the false rumor of Madalyn Murray O'Hare's petition against religious broadcasting, these stories seem to be spread just to make Christians appear gullible.

Satan delights in making Christians expend time and energy chasing "silly myths" (1 Tim. 4:7). The rock group Petra cleverly describes their problem in the tune, "Witch Hunt": "Looking for evil wherever we can find it/ Off on a tangent, hope the Lord won't mind it/ Another Witch Hunt, takin' a break from all our gospel labor/ On a crusade but we forgot our saber."

The "saber" to which Petra refers is the sword of truth. We all need to employ it regularly if we're going to "avoid stupid controversies . . . for they are unprofitable and futile" (Titus 3:9, RSV). We must learn to cut through the mountains of information that come our way and discern what is true and vital to our Christian walk.

---

[1]Frank Gaebelein, "The Christian, The Arts, And Truth," (Portland, Oreg.: Multnomah, 1985), p. 67.

So let's examine the "African beat" story as if some version of the tale were true. Misinterpretations sometimes occur when we attempt to understand other cultures, so if natives were observed associating rock's beat with their culture's demon-conjuring music, the mistake is understandable. There are, after all, certain superficial similarities in rhythm and drum sounds. More importantly, the natives would have nothing else with which to compare it. Similarly, if we—with our Western cultural biases—were to see two Middle Eastern men embracing, we could easily mistake their intentions.

Secondly, while a heavy drumbeat accompanies music utilized for devil worship, that doesn't automatically cast an evil shadow over the beat or the drums. After all, the ancient Egyptians worshiped their false gods with the same rhythmic beating of timbrels Miriam and the Hebrew women used in celebration of God's saving power. Did the superficial similarities cast suspicion on the worship? No. Their intent took precedence over any similarity to pagan methods of expression.

Likewise, both Jerry Lee Lewis and his cousin, Jimmy Swaggart, utilize a juke-joint rhythm and style in much of their music. Their lyrics are different, but their sound is often very similar—white, southern rockabilly. Since Lewis claims to be singing "devil music," is Swaggart then guilty by association? No, the heart of the performer, not the superficial similarities, makes the difference.

Or let's look outside music for another example. In the sports world, football is the object of millions of dollars of betting. Does this misuse of the sport, illegal gambling for selfish gain, make the football an evil object which Christians may not use or enjoy? Of course not. Does the use of the typewriter and printing press for the writing and producing of pornography make such devices evil, unusable for Christian work? Of course not. Neither does the use of a drum beat to conjure up evil somehow magically dirty the use of the same sound for righteous purposes.

Finally, let's bury the false notion that African music is primitive. If introduced to the many varieties of African music, even the most tinny ear could recognize the complex nature of the rhythms and the intricate multi-part harmonies of indigenous

African music. To maintain otherwise veers us dangerously close to ignorant racism that writer Studs Terkel terms "a nineteenth century lie which becomes a twentieth century obscenity."

But what does God say about the beat in music? Doesn't Christian rock music use a "devil's beat" that God would find displeasing?

We find it interesting that some of the same people who condemn Christian rock's thumping beat as "devil's music" will clap their hands in the very same syncopated rhythm while enjoying an ol' time gospel tune or watching an old-fashioned country square dance. Every composer who has ever lived has worked with time and rhythm. It's created by God and it's part of our very natures. Bach and rock each employ rhythm, though the beat is more often very pronounced in rock music. But the metronome has been in use for a long, long time and its whole purpose is to click off a set of mathematical intervals on which the music is structured.

Throughout biblical history, notably in the days of Saul and David, many percussion instruments—from drums to cymbals to castanets—were used by God's chosen people. The use of these rhythm instruments is recorded in the Psalms, yet, the Bible says nothing negative about the beat these devices must have lent to the performance of the Psalms. If God has chosen to ignore the issue of beat, dare we make arbitrary rulings?

"We've had the mistaken impression for too long that somehow the Creator doesn't have rhythm," maintains Grammy award-winning trumpet player Phil Driscoll. "God is the King of soul; He's the King of all rhythm."[2]

You say music should not disturb inner peace, and yet, when I hear the rock-y Christian music my son plays, I feel very agitated.

In his letter to the Romans, Paul exhorts to "pursue what makes for peace," reminding those who have a greater sense of freedom to keep that liberty personal—"between yourself and God" (14:19–22, RSV). He realized one person's stumbling block might not disturb the peace of another, so discernment is a very personal process.

---

[2]Davin Seay, "The Marvelous Music Maker," *Charisma* (2/86), p. 40.

Music, by its very nature, produces very individual associations. In fact, because we associate music so strongly with events from our own past, music is sometimes used to help amnesia victims recall names, ideas, and mental pictures. Musical therapist Nancy Hunt claims music is an extremely powerful tool, both physically and psychologically: "It can make us relax, or remember, or to have all sorts of feelings. It all depends on what we project onto the music."[3]

But not everyone projects the same associations onto the same music. Therefore, one person's heavenly hymn might be another's dreadful dirge. Richard D. Mountford, professor of music at Malone College in Canton, Ohio, explains, "Highly personal associations can emerge when we hear music which we encounter at a time of emotional stress or exhilaration. Psychologists call such an association 'classical conditioning' or 'signal learning.' . . . This conditioning is resistant to our efforts to be free of it, and Christians must be conscious of its effects upon them."[4]

One Christian rock fan wrote to *Contemporary Christian* magazine of his personal struggle with musical associations: "Sometimes I have to ask myself if a particular song or group draws me closer to God or closer to the world. . . . Some groups' music makes me want to get high on drugs again."

Likewise, a writer to our ministry confessed, "When I listen to hard music, be it rock or Christian rock, my sinful nature strongly comes to the surface. It reminds me of the pleasures of sin when I was into drugs and living for the Devil."

In both cases, links with the past make it doubtful whether these Christians should listen to any form of rock music. At the same time, we musn't draw the conclusion that the music produced their drug urges. Instead, the temptations probably came from their past experiences and feelings which often were accompanied by mainstream rock music.

We should pay close attention to any negative associations we have with music. And if the associations we connect with certain songs or styles incite sinful thoughts, or dredge up best-forgotten

---

[3]Gale Maleskey, "Music That Strikes a Healing Chord," *Prevention* (10/83), p. 58.
[4]Richard D. Mountford, "Does the Music Make Them Do It?" *Christianity Today* (5/4/79), p. 22.

memories, or inspire melancholy moods, then we should avoid that music—no matter what style it is.

At the same time, we should remember that Romans 14 reminds us not to pass judgment on others simply because they have differing views. In the passage, Paul speaks of, among other things, eating meat offered to idols (a practice which was dividing Roman Christians). But we can easily substitute music in the text, and see the same principles apply (the substitutions are in parentheses):

> One person's faith allows him to [listen to] any [style of Christian music], but the person who is weak in the faith [listens only to "sacred" music]. The person who will [listen to any kind of Christian music] is not to despise the one who doesn't; while the one who [listens only to hymns] is not to pass judgment on the one who will [listen to Christian rock]; for God has accepted him. . . . One person thinks that a certain [style of music] is more important than other [styles], while someone else thinks that all [styles of music] are the same. Each one should firmly make up his own mind. . . . Everyone of us, then, will have to give an account of himself to God. [Paraphrased from Rom. 14:2–12, GNB]

Paul is implying we should not judge another's music by the associations it creates in our mind. Nevertheless, many older adults tell us they won't let their children listen to music similar to big band era tunes, because the music stirs up memories of the dance halls and the loose living they were involved in before they came to know Christ. Other parents are offended by any country-style music—even if it is Christian—because they associate it with the bar scene and the immoral lifestyle they led before they made a commitment to Jesus. Therefore, they forbade their children to hear anything sounding like country-style.

We appreciate parents who get involved and care about the music their youngsters listen to, and we support their efforts to guide their children's understanding of music. At the same time, we hope they remember not to take for granted that what is bad for them is automatically bad for their children.

If our teenagers listen consistently to music which makes us uncomfortable, the best thing we can do is talk about it, telling them how the music affects us and why, asking what effect the music has on them, and talking about the associations that can accompany music. We thus can work together toward an understanding of what is best for everyone, unafraid to admit we have differences. As we stated in the chapter on "shalts and shalt nots," parents do have the last word. However, this makes them responsible for making wise, informed judgments.

You condemned Donna Summer in Why Knock Rock? Do you recommend her now that she's a Christian? And what about Bob Dylan whom you recommended earlier? Now do you condemn him?

Our purpose in *Why Knock Rock?* was not specifically to condemn anyone, but to offer information, culled from hours of research, which would reveal the lyrics, lifestyles, goals and graphics of popular secular artists. Unfortunately, many rock stars live such seamy lives or sing such rotten lyrics that they literally prove themselves guilty. But not all secular artists are evil, any more than all Christian artists are good—that's oversimplifying things.

Furthermore, people change—sometimes for the better, sometimes for the worse. But not everything Summer sang (before her renewed commitment to God) was bad, any more than everything she sings now is good. And the same is true for every artist—including Bob Dylan.

Once again, that's why we don't award a Peters Brothers' Seal of Approval. We concur with John Fischer's assessment: "Mature people don't need to wait for someone else to put labels all over their world. They can separate good from evil"[5] Therefore, we encourage you to use the criteria we've established and decide for yourself. With just a touch of skepticism, constantly reevaluate your music and your favorite artists. By that we mean, try to remain detached in your appraisal, and always check for fruit.

A number of Christian groups are now appearing in clubs and bars and other secular venues. Would you advise them to do so?

When Christian musicians play the secular club circuit, they are often criticized for appearing in sinful settings. And we have

---

[5]John Fischer, "Wrong Rock, Right Roll," *Campus Life* (M-22), p. 84.

to admit, we have some serious doubts about the advisability of doing so unless a group is both spiritually mature and sure of a genuine call from the Lord to do so.

However, Jesus was attacked for the same reason, and He wasn't afraid to take His message anywhere. He knew the world had no power over Him. Likewise, it has no power over us unless we allow it. Nevertheless, some Christians think that because the "days are evil," we should stay away from such places. This separationist view seems quite ludicrous if we realize that we don't censure Christian journalists who infiltrate the secular media, or Christian athletes who achieve fame in the sports world. So why single out Christian musicians?

In fact, though we are to avoid companions and surroundings that produce temptation for us, Jesus never said to associate only with our own. He not only wants us to follow His example, He commands us to go. Concerning this command, Paul challenges, "How are they to believe in him of whom they have never heard? And how are they to hear without a preacher? And how can men preach unless they are sent? As it is written, 'How beautiful are the feet of those who preach good news!' " (Rom. 10:14, 15, RSV).

Preaching the Good News can be a tough calling, but how can we deny to others the treasure we have? Though singing in the secular marketplace is a much more difficult route to go, and the temptations are high, we contend, as lyricist/music producer Mike States does, "So many American Christian groups seem content to be isolationists, happy to make a comfortable living playing songs about Christ to audiences who are already convinced. . . . Since the church is simply the body of believers, let's take the church into the pubs and clubs and bars and let them hear the other side, the correct side, the truth!"[6]

Christian musicians who invade those pubs and clubs need our support just as much as any missionary away from the flock. If Christian entertainers choose to spread the Good News (as the old evangelists used to say) "on the front porch of hell," let's send them out with ears full of cheerful approval and pockets full of prayers.

---

[6]Mike States, "The States Report," *New Christian Media* (Vol. 3: No. 4).

The Bible says, "Be ye separate" (2 Cor. 6:17). In light of that command, what's your opinion of artists who "cross over" into secular music?

The apostle Paul was writing to Christians in a society proud of its moral depravity. Common pagan cultic practices—including religious prostitution—were difficult for the new Christians to shake. Consequently, they made numerous mistakes. They fell into sin, apostasy and factions. Out of concern, Paul cautioned believers to stay away from people who were a bad influence on them, those who would persuade them back into old habits, old pagan beliefs.

We also live in a depraved society, and Paul's message is just as applicable to us as it was to the believers in Corinth. However, we need to heed him correctly. Paul is saying we should avoid partnership with the world, which means participation in immoral activity.

Since music is not a sinful pursuit, there is no biblical basis for the assumption that a Christian artist in the secular marketplace is compromising his faith. Granted, the secular music world has its share of temptations, but certainly some artists must be strong enough to go forth as "standard bearers" in the midst of evil. Is there no one who can answer Jeremiah's call to "assemble and . . . go into the fortified cities," to "raise a standard for Zion"? (Jer. 4:5, 6, RSV). Likewise, Paul was not saying we should develop sinnerphobia, but that we should avoid joining in their sinful pursuits. If we were to cordon ourselves off entirely from this world, how could we hope to be "salt" or "light" to the unsaved? We therefore have no problems with Christian artists' efforts to reach a broader market.

Charles "Scott" Ross, who has worked in the Christian media for more than 15 years, sees a need for Christians willing—and able—to tackle the issues of the day in a manner to which the world can relate. "As I've turned on Christian radio recently," he claims, "I hear so much talk about the Antichrist, the Rapture, the Four Horsemen. Then I come home and fight with my wife, or my kid bites me on the kneecap, or I get laid off my job after 20 years. What does pie-in-the-sky theology have to do with such problems? Jesus dealt with practical issues. We need practical answers."[7]

Artists attempting to find a spot in the secular marketplace will often find themselves in challenging situations, and Satan would like nothing better than to destroy such a visible witness. Therefore, artists must constantly strive to "walk as children of light" and "try to learn what is pleasing to the Lord. Take no part in the unfruitful works of darkness, but instead expose them. . . . Look carefully then how you walk, not as unwise men but as wise, making the most of the time, because the days are evil" (Eph. 5:8–15, RSV).

I am surprised, indeed shocked, that you recommend music such as "Christian" rock, heavy metal, new-wave or jazz-rock fusion. How can you condone those evil styles by labeling them "Christian"?

As stated throughout this book, we think the Bible doesn't categorize music, except where intentions are concerned. It neither discusses style nor declares certain styles dangerous. Therefore, labeling music Christian rock or Christian heavy metal is simply giving the music descriptive titles to which young people can relate.

We can understand the aversion to using secular terms to describe different styles of music, though. It's natural to associate the style's name with the secular version. Even we first think of Twisted Sister obscenities, Iron Maiden monstrosities and Black Sabbath satanism when we hear the term "heavy metal," but that's just our cultural conditioning.

Similarly, one might mistake a modern Christian romance novel—because of its genre title—with the sordid, sex-filled stories peddled by so many secular publishers. In truth, the book could well provide a faith-building, uplifting story of genuine Christian love, but unfortunately, there is no term but "romance" that will describe this style of book.

In the same way, musical styles are difficult to describe without using commonly accepted terminology. And even if we invented better terms to describe the music, how would anyone

---

[7]Joe Polizzi, "Radio Rap," *Christian Contemporary* (4/83), p. 29.

know what style we were talking about? Therefore, let's just agree not to be frightened away by labels.

Besides, if enough Christian heavy metal artists become popular, heavy metal could soon be connected with throwing Bibles into the audiences instead of beer bottles onto the stage! Despite our past associations with rock music terms, let's grant Christian musicians the freedom to attempt to redeem the music market place.

I have heard that the beat, or rhythm, of a song appeals to the flesh, the melody to the spirit and the harmony to the soul. If so, doesn't "Christian" rock's strong beat overpower the melody and harmony, and appeal to fleshly desires?

We've heard variations on this beat-harmony-melody theme from literally scores of sources. Most show little apparent concern for the reliability (or biblical basis) of the so-called documentation. Presumably, one 'authority' has gotten it from another, who's gotten it from another, *ad nauseum*. We did, however, come across one foe of contemporary music who, though misquoting his source, revealed the author of the concept: Pythagorus. But the author failed to look deeper into what Pythagorus actually believed.

Although Pythagorus left no writings, he had a major influence on ancient Greek thought. His advanced thinking earned him recognition as the founder of arithmetic and geometry, and the father of science.[8] His credits include the discovery of the earth's spherical shape, the formula for the dimensions of a right triangle, and a mathematical understanding of the notes of the musical scale.[9] In addition, he inspired a large group of followers, called Pythagoreans, who considered their founder an immortal pseudo-Christ, a son of God.[10]

The Pythagoreans are recognized for two main beliefs: Rein-

[8]James Hastings, ed., *Encyclopedia of Religion and Ethics* (New York: Charles Scribner's Sons, 1955), pp. 520, 527, 529.

[9]Donald Jay Grout, *A History of Western Music: Revised Edition* (New York: W.W. Norton, 1973), p. 27.

[10]Manly Hall, *Encyclopedic Outline of Masonic, Hermetic, Qabbalistic and Rosicrucian Symbolical Philosphy* (Los Angeles: Philosophical Research Society, 1928), p. LXV.

carnation, or the transmigration of souls, and a concept "that numbers constitute the true nature of things."[11] These doctrines rose from Pythagorus' belief that God was the Monad, "the One that is Everything. . . . the Supreme Mind distributed throughout all parts of the universe. . . ."[12] In other words, Pythagorus was a pantheist. He probably also was an occultist, familiar with mystery religions of Egypt, Babylon, etc., and thus practiced divination, as well as numerology.[13]

As part of his pantheistic view, Pythagorus believed "the planets and stars were merely bodies encasing souls, minds, and spirits. . . ."[14] And to season his brew of a "live" universe based on numbers, he mixed in music. Geometry and music, he believed, were the bases for astronomy.[15] He was convinced the heavenly bodies were spaced according to the numerical values of the musical scale, as if arranged at appropriate points along a single string of an instrument.[16] This "harmony of the spheres" produced musical tones which an "in tune" soul could hear![17]

These concepts promoted by Pythagorus disagree not only with the Bible, but with modern science as well. As Manly Hall, a student of mystical religion, warns, these ideas are based wholly on "ancient beliefs of the nature and structure of the world and not according to the attitudes and opinions which prevail in modern time."[18] Thus Pythagorus' views of the nature of man and the universe deserve great skepticism. They seem amazingly similar to the worldly wisdom Paul warned about: "See to it that no one makes a prey of you by philosophy and empty deceit, according to human tradition, according to the elemental spirits of the universe, and not according to Christ" (Col. 2:8, 23, RSV).

So what about Pythagorus and rock music? He stressed, con-

---

[11]William H. Harris and Judith Levey, eds., *New Columbia* Encyclopedia (New York: Columbia University Press, 1975), p. 2553.

[12]Hall, *Encyclopedic Outline*, p. LXVI.

[13]Ibid., pp. LXV, LXVII, LXIX.

[14]Ibid., p. LXVI.

[15]Ibid. p. LXX.

[16]Manly P. Hall, *Therapeutic Value of Music Including the Philosophy of Music* (Los Angeles: Philosophical Research Society, 1982), p. 54.

[17]Hastings, p. 528.

[18]Hall, *Therapeutic Value of Music*, p. 55.

sistent with ancient Greek views, that music contained three elements: rhythm, melody, and harmony—which must always remain in balance.[19] Otherwise, the listener and the entire solar system could be affected.

Rhythm, he purported, affected the flesh, though his term for "flesh" didn't connote sensuality. It simply meant the physical body. However, there is no biblical support for the conclusion that songs which affect us physically are sinful. The notion of physical experience as evil is an ancient heresy that periodically rears its ugly head like a Lock Ness phantom. If God had desired that we have no physical sensations, why did He give us bodies? Why did He give His Son a body?

Melody, Pythagorus thought, was associated with the soul or psyche—which we would term thoughts and feelings. Although melody does prompt emotional responses, we are convinced lyrics and personal associations with music, as well as other important elements, have a more profound effect on us. But Pythagorus oversimplifies. Melody and rhythm are inseparable, for without rhythm, melody is dead. Consequently, a belief that rhythm affects the body and melody the soul is inaccurate. Each affects both.

The Pythagorean view of *harmony*, however, is the most disturbing. He maintained harmony affects the spirit—a theory that fits his pantheistic view of a musical universe. Others have held similar beliefs. Hindus believed instant enlightenment was possible if one could but precisely strike the right musical chord. Likewise, God is supposed to embody the tone made through the chanting of the Sanskrit word "om." In contrast, medieval church musicians avoided an augmented fourth (or diminished fifth) chord because they believed the devil possessed that sound.

All this sounds like hocus-pocus to our modern Western ears—so why have so many of us readily swallowed an ancient Greek philosophy of music's effect on a person (sometimes in a slightly modified version that reverses the role of spirit and soul)? If harmony alone makes the spirit soar, then is three-part harmony less spiritual than four-part harmony? If harmony is the

---

[19]Ibid., p. 17.

only aspect of music which affects the spirit, did Paul's encouragement of the Ephesians to "address one another in psalms, hymns and spiritual songs" puzzle them? How did they sing "spiritual songs" when harmony, as we know it, was not in use? And since Hebrew music during David's time was also monophonic (without harmony), did the Psalms he penned affect only the flesh and the mind?

If we really want to take Pythagorus seriously, we must use stringed instruments exclusively (which would include the guitar), because only these could copy the perfect harmony of the universe. Pythagorus insisted his disciples stay away from any music made by wind or percussion instruments.[20] So let's delete Psalm 150's trumpet, timbrel, flute and cymbals! And cut out all biblical references to the trumpet—over fifty of them! And take our children out of the school band! And discard our Sousa records! All because of Pythagorus.

To accept these ideas based on what appears to be mystical, superstitious "philosophies of men" seems a dangerous mistake. On the surface, they may sound and look good, but what is the basis for the conclusions drawn? Should not our basis for thoughtful decisions in all areas of life—including music—be the Scriptures, not philosophies based on a pantheistic view of the universe? Should we allow our religious attitudes toward music to be governed, not by fact or even theory, but unproven ancient hypothesis, mere conjecture? We believe Christians have a higher authority, who encourages virtually any style of music performed in His honor.

---

[20]Ibid., p. 63.

Chapter Twelve

An Open Letter to Christian Artists

I don't think the Devil's gonna ever forgive me for what I'm doing.

—*Carman*

Dear Brothers and Sisters,

Researching this book has been a great pleasure. As we've attended and enjoyed your concerts and festivals, and interviewed you in person or over the phone, we've come to know you in a surprisingly personal sense. We've met your families and surveyed the backstage scene. We've waited until very late at night to speak to you sometimes, because you were with fans after the show, counseling, praying, laughing, crying. We've watched some of you go onstage and give a fine performance, despite bad weather, a bout with the flu, or recent surgery. Of course, we're generalizing, but we were favorably impressed with the people involved in Christian contemporary music!

We have also seen some things we don't agree with and have met a few people we felt were making some mistakes. We care about you and we're concerned about your welfare and the welfare of your fans. With that in mind, we'd like to offer a few suggestions for you to consider as you go about your work for the Lord. Please take them in the spirit in which they are given—as loving thoughts from your friends.

1. Point them to God. Scripture makes it clear that God is the source of any success we have—"In Him we live and move and have our being" (Acts 17:28, RSV); " . . . for apart from me you can do nothing" (John 15:5, RSV).

Please, friend, don't be swept away by holy hype. Resist the temptation to believe your own press releases. Don't ever forget the Source of your talents. "Every creative shred of your body is there because of the Lord," Pastor Don Finto reminds us. "All your talent is from Him. Every gift you have comes from Him. Every line of lyric, every melody, every intonation of voice—He makes it all possible. Your creative juices are His alone."

The apostle Paul writes on the same theme, "Who sees anything different in you? What have you that you did not receive? If then you received it, why do you boast as if it were not a gift?" (1 Cor. 4:7, RSV). Don't allow the spotlights and the applause to fool you. Don't ever forget you are made in God's creative image. He alone is responsible for your talent.

It's important for your own well-being that you recognize where your gifts come from, but your fans also need to see more than a gifted artist when they watch you perform. "I was reading through Psalm 87 one day," Finto notes, "and it said, 'As they make music they will see all my talents.' And I thought, *People always sing; let's help them sing to the Lord. Let's point them to the Lord.*"

2. Don't be drawn away from the love of God by your love of music.
In *The Great Divorce*, C. S. Lewis envisions people who have died and gone to hell and how they would respond if offered a chance to repent. One character—an artist—is allowed to visit heaven, but rather than learning to appreciate it, he only sees heaven as scenery subjects to paint. He can only experience it through his art. His spirit guide reminds him, however, "You're forgetting. That is not how you began. Light itself was your first love: you loved paint only as a means of telling about light."

The spirit warns the artist of the trap in which he is ensnared. "Every poet and musician and artist, but for grace, is drawn away from love of the thing he tells, to love of the telling, till down in Deep Hell, they cannot be interested in God at all but only in what they say about Him. For it doesn't stop at being interested in paint, you know. They sink lower—become interested in their own personalities and then in nothing but their own reputations."

As you pursue your musical goals, ask God to keep you safe from the sin of the builders of Babel (Gen. 11). Their pride was not in the Lord, but in their building skills. They built their tower, not to reach God, but to make a name, a reputation, for themselves. Be sure you don't ever get so caught up in your music, or your goals, or yourself, or your popularity that you forget the Lord. Seek Him out daily. Spend time with Him. Aim to always hold God closer to your heart than your music. You are the singer; let Him be your song.

3. Be clear and consistent in your message. Don't ever compromise your message. By that, we don't mean your music must always be a gospel message, but it must always contain gospel truth. Whether you sing to the sinner or the saved, never settle for second-hand emotions and phony testimony. It's so easy to fall into a Christian-cheerleader mode, performing songs that, as songwriter Greg Nelson says, "honor men and encourage God, instead of honoring God and encouraging men."

But resist the temptation to sugar coat that "old, old, story." Tell it perhaps in new ways, but always tell it like it is. David Hazard, a respected editor-writer cautions, "We must never confuse our desire for people to accept the gospel with creating a gospel that is acceptable to people."[1] Whether the subject is love, ethics, war, suicide, sin or God himself, be sure your music isn't saying only what you think people want to hear, but what God would want them to hear.

Keep close to your heart the admonition in 2 Corinthians 4:1–2: "It is God himself, in his mercy, who has given us this wonderful work [of telling his Good News to others], and so we . . . do not try to trick people into believing—we are not interested in fooling anyone. We never try to get anyone to believe that the Bible teaches what it doesn't" (TLB).

When David was fighting Saul for the kingdom, he called for soldiers, but he also called for people who "had understanding of the times, to know what Israel ought to do" (1 Chron. 12:32). In the same way, the world today cries for answers. We sorely need Christians who understand the source of the world's trou-

---

[1]David Hazard, "Holy Hype," *Eternity* (12/85), p. 41.

ble and know what to do about it.

As artists, you have an opportunity to influence our society tremendously, so don't waste your talent answering questions no one is asking. Don't use in-house God-talk. Instead, make every word count. Stir your listeners to compassion. Challenge them to action. Fire them with the Spirit. Inspire them with hope and faith. Warn them of the world's dangers. Remind them of the suffering of others. Heal them with messages of God's peace. Draw them together in love. Through your music, provide a light to those in darkness.

4. Stay in close fellowship with others. Paul speaks of some of his peers who measure themselves by their own standards or by comparisons within their own circle, which, he concludes, doesn't make for accurate estimation (2 Cor. 10:12). The Apostle might be speaking to you as well. Does your hectic lifestyle and busy time on the road tempt you to seek fellowship only with your traveling companions, rather than a larger church body? To do so may warp your vision. You may no longer see things accurately and both your music and your ministry may be affected.

Word Record's executive director, Neal Joseph, says, "Each artist has to have a home church they are in contact with. A group that supports them whether they are there on Sunday or not. They need to have a board of people—ministers to lay people to businessmen—to help them with their ministries and lives and careers.

"When out on the road, perspective gets warped, it's not the real world. Artists need a group of people to spend time with, to help them make decisions. That's how they can maintain contact. That's how they can remain accountable."

Artist manager Wes Yoder echoes the same concerns, "One of the things I would like to see is more Christian artists accountable to the local structure of the body of Christ. They are not as involved as they ought to be. All of a sudden they're feeling alone. If disasters come around in their lives, they have no one to turn to. It's just a very difficult thing."

Please build around yourself a support system of loving people who know you well and can help shoulder the burdens and responsibilities that come with a public life. Don't think you are invincible. As we have warned before, Satan would love to destroy the public witness of any artist trying to live a sold-out life for the Lord. Fellowship with a local body—as Steve Taylor says, with people who are not impressed with your celebrity—is like mandatory "Life insurance" for your ministry. Don't leave home without it.

5. *Don't be surprised by adversity.* As a Christian on the front lines battling for our culture, don't be too surprised if others misunderstand. As George Verwer reminds us, "Pharisee-ism is still a major religious cause." There will be those who disagree with what you are doing, and they may attack you for it.

And Satan will use those things to discourage you. He wants your work stopped. He'll tempt you to give up not only your ministry but your walk with the Lord. Making Satan an enemy is part of the price you pay for the privilege of ministry, says the evangelical entertainer, Carman—"I don't think the Devil's ever gonna forgive me for what I'm doing," he told *Contemporary Christian* magazine.

Carman has a point, but don't be surprised by adversity, or let undue criticism get you down. No one is so big as to avoid it. Thomas à Kempis once said, "Do not concern thyself overmuch about who is for thee or against thee; but take care to act so that God will be with thee in everything that thou doest. Keep clean thy conscience, and God will defend thee, for he that receiveth the protection of God, no man's malice shall be able to harm."

Take out the "thees" and "thous" and you have, "Sticks and stones can hurt my bones, but with the Lord, words will never harm me." So walk closely with God. Keep your eyes on Him and declare war on discouragement. Find your rest, as well as your affirmation, in Him. He will give you the spiritual "eyes" needed to keep things in balance.

6. *Beware of the pitfall of hero worship.* Kansas sings, "Everybody falls in love with the main attraction. . . . They all want to know/ What's it like to be a rock star?" We all tend to want celebrities to be bigger-than-life pedestal people. We allow the stage smoke to cover flaws, and the bright lights to blind us to frailties.

Though you can utilize your position of power to bring others to Christ, the hero worship that sometimes comes with public life can be a dangerous pitfall. In a candid assessment of Christian contemporary music, Keith Green once admitted that even he was sometimes offended by the spiritual posturing of some Christian artists: "It is not the beat that offends me, not the volume—it's the spirit. It's the 'Look at me!' attitude I have seen in concert after concert"[2]

Unlikely though it may seem, Barnabus and Paul dealt with the same sort of hero worship in Lystra; however, they were able to resist the "look at me" urge. There they healed a grateful cripple and word soon spread that they were gods come to earth. The crowds gave them the names of gods and prepared to offer sacrifices to them, but Paul and Barnabus let neither their success nor the fame that followed it to go to their heads.

First, they were honest about themselves. "We are merely human beings like yourselves!" they exclaimed. Then they gently redirected the acclaim to the Source of their gifts. "We have come to bring you the Good News that you are invited to turn from the worship of these foolish things and to pray instead to the living God. . ." (Acts 14:15, TLB).

A useful saying says, "To handle yourself, use your head; to handle others, use your heart." In other words, when dealing with yourself, stick with facts, not with feelings. When dealing with others, be compassionate, feel what they feel. It's a good guide for anyone leading a public lifestyle—any public lifestyle—to follow. Don't get carried away by media attention, swallowed up by success until there's nothing real left of you. Keep a cool head—you know who and what you really are. Don't allow success to go to your head, making you "puffed up without reason" (Col. 2:18, RSV).

We saw so many of you care for your fans with such affection and consideration, perhaps we don't need to remind you, but be sure to treat them as warmly and humanly as you would like to be treated. Steer them, as much as possible, away from the star routine of pictures and autographs and allow them to see you as

---

[2]Pretty Good Printing, Last Days Ministries, Lindale, TX.

you really are. Make Paul's attitude your own: "We don't go around preaching about ourselves, but about Jesus Christ as Lord. All we say of ourselves is that we are your slaves because of what Jesus has done for us" (2 Cor. 4:5, TLB).

7. Take neither success nor the apparent lack of it too seriously. Record sales, recording contracts, applause, media hype and radio airplay—are those indicators of your success? We hope not. Though the business end of things has to be handled realistically, and with good stewardship, don't view it as a barometer of success or failure. Though it's wonderful when financial success occurs, God makes no guarantees. Sometimes the success He blesses us with isn't immediately apparent. So just as fans need to look at the fruit of your ministry in their discernment process, you need to look for fruit, not record sales.

Likewise, when success does come, remember fame is not only fleeting, it is also very fickle. "I've always loved the passage," divulges Calvin Miller, "that says, 'Jesus knew the heart of man.' He knew what was in the heart—He knew the fickleness of the audience. To be paraded through the streets as a hero on Sunday, and to be crucified on Thursday night; He understood that."

Let's be honest, will you and your work even be recognized by the public in the next century? In twenty years? In ten years? Tomorrow? Maybe not. But the antidote to the world's fickleness, says Miller, is never to take success too seriously. "Any artist who succeeds real fast, who is immediately popular, probably needs to realize that most quick successes are not very long-lived." If you are immediately popular—wonderful. However, don't gauge your success on your instant popularity. For many, their instant fame was their downfall. Don't let yourself get caught up in the hype. Instead, remember your real goals, and gauge your success on whether or not you are attaining them.

8. Work to become, not to acquire. Several years ago a tongue-in-cheek little book, *The Yuppie Handbook,* caused a minor sensation when it detailed the goals of the new generation of American materialists termed "Yuppies" (Young Urban Professionals). The book's humor lay in its closeness to reality as it poked fun at our absurd, materialistic goals: "glory, prestige, recognition, fame, social status, power, money or any and all combinations of the above."

While such blessings as recognition, power and money are not evil in themselves, they make poor—if not dangerous—goals. For with these false goals, you may become as the false teachers Jude spoke of, "like clouds ... without ... rain," promising much, but producing nothing (Jude 1:12, TLB).

In contrast, Jesus stands as a perfect example of goal setting and seeking. The celebrity-conscious people of His day wanted to make Him a superstar in much the same way as we do to rock stars today. His fans would have succeeded had not Jesus' goals been different. It's no accident He shunned power and status. His eye was always on a more lasting goal. There was no confusion in His mind about what He wanted to do and why. Jesus was not about acquiring wealth, fame or military power. He was about being our Savior.

Though success and fame, money and power may come your way, don't let them fill your dreams or become your motivating force. Strive for something more. Let your first goal be to become all God has in mind for you, to "love the Lord your God with all your heart, soul, and mind," and to "love your neighbor as much as you love yourself" (Matt. 22:37–40, TLB).

Working within this framework, you'll be free to rightly use your talent in many ways. And you'll also be able to formulate any number of secondary goals: evangelism, encouragement, social commentary, entertainment, whatever. On the contrary, if you aren't willing to "become" first, you'll have little of real value to offer those who look to you as a role model. Also, publicly state those secondary goals. Not only will it help you to better target your music, it assists people in matching their needs to your music, and helps avoid misunderstandings.

9. Sing not for your supper, nor solely for men's souls. Sing for God's pleasure. One well-known evangelist who is categorically against Christian rock music, claims, "If Christian rock was not selling so many records, if it didn't pack the concerts, if it didn't produce such idolizing of the performers—it would die almost overnight. . . . It's all a matter of big bucks! Popularity! Climbing the charts! Big crowds!"

While we strongly disagree with this writer's assessment of Christian music, we do want to remind you of your purpose. God made you and gave you talents and gifts, not so you would win the world's acclaim and applause, but primarily so you would use them for His pleasure.

In *Chariots of Fire*, when the great Olympic runner, Eric Liddell, was asked by his sister why he was dedicating himself to running, he said, "God made me for a purpose, but he also made me fast. And when I run, I feel His pleasure."

In the same way, your highest goal is to perfect and perform your craft for God's pleasure. While you create music—for entertainment, edification, or any purpose—don't ask yourself, Will this song be a commercial success? Or even, Does this song have a clear evangelistic message? God's desire is simply that you obey and do your best. He is your first, your foremost audience. When you do what God has created you to do, you bring Him pleasure. Then the questions are much simpler: Is this my best? Am I as creative as I know how to be? When I play my music, do I feel His pleasure?

When you feel His pleasure, then you will be free to meet the challenge of William Booth, the founder of the Salvation Army, who proclaimed, "Every note, every strain, and every harmony is divine and belongs to us . . . bring out your cornets and harps and organs and flutes and violins and pianos and drums, and everything else that can make a melody. Offer them to God, and use them to make all the hearts about you merry before the Lord" (C. Barnes, *God's Army*, p. 100).

So bring out your instruments. Play your tunes. Feel God's pleasure. And make our hearts merry in the process!

> God's blessing on you and
> your music,
> Dan and Steve Peters
> Cher Merrill

"Let them praise his name with dancing, making melody to him with timbrel and lyre! For the Lord takes pleasure in his people."

—Psalm 149:3–4, RSV

The Ten Most Needed List

"I bet I read one hundred letters from kids saying, 'Praise God, you're saved. We've been praying for you for years.' I got prayed into the Kingdom!"

—*Kerry Livgren, A.D.*

In *Why Knock Rock?*, we included rock and roll's "Ten Most Wanted List." Rather than condemning rock artists, we suggested concerned people pray for them, write to them and give them an opportunity to meet the Lord.

Kerry Livgren, formerly of the mainstream rock group Kansas, admonishes, "Never give up hope and don't think that because someone is a high and lofty person in the world—a rock star or a government leader or whatever—that they are beyond your prayers."

As a born-again Christian, Livgren, who now fronts the Christian group A.D., adds, "When I became a Christian and it became public knowledge that I'd been converted, I started getting literally hundreds of letters. I got mail bags full of letters. And the first time I opened up one of those bags of letters, I started reading those letters and began weeping uncontrollably because I read at least one hundred letters—one after another—from kids saying, 'Praise God, you're saved. We've been praying for you for years!' I got prayed into the Kingdom!"

Livgren's story is, of course, very encouraging. God listens to our prayers for these people. However, his story also made us wonder how many of those same fans are praying for Livgren now. It's often said the devil doesn't bother with sinners—he knows their fate; instead, he works hardest on the saved. How much more must he want the spiritual destruction of Christian artists who have so much potential for positively influencing our young people.

Repeatedly, artists we interview say they desire our prayers. Some are experiencing financial difficulties. Said one performer, "It has been such a hard year that we thought this might be the end. Finances fell through, and we went four months this year without being paid. . . . We're just believing God that we are where He wants us to be and He's going to take care of all things."

Others are suffering attacks from well-meaning but misunderstanding Christians. One artist pleaded, "If someone has problems with Christian rock, if it's not 'of God' in their eyes, then [tell them to] pray for us, not condemn us or attack our ministries. Pray for us that we would be able to hear God better and know what He wants us to do."

The fact that no one is immune to temptation, and that Christian rock music's performers need our prayerful support was never more apparent than in the fall of 1985, when one member of a prominent Christian group was convicted of child molestation. In heartfelt response, the rest of the group explained they had no previous knowledge of the problem, then issued this plea: "There are, quite frankly, some deep emotional scars. We thank God because He heals and forgives all of us, and that His Spirit rekindles the spirit of hope and courage. . . . Now we need your prayers more than ever. The issues of today are serious. Let us pray for the wisdom, grace and strength of our Father so that we can respond to these issues of today with the compassion and love of our Saviour."

Below we list ten of Christian contemporary music's most influential artists, performers likely to touch countless lives for the Lord. For that reason alone, Satan would take great pleasure in destroying their witness. In a spirit of love, then, let's agree to keep them surrounded by prayer, and also let them know they are being supported. But let's also not forget to pray for all Christian entertainers that God would, as Amy Grant sings, keep His angels watching over them.

1. *De Garmo and Key*, c/o Brock and Associates, P.O. Box 14543, Oklahoma City, OK 73113.

2. *Amy Grant*, Friends of Amy, P.O. Box 50701, Nashville, TN 37205.

3. *Stryper*, P.O. Box 1045, Cypress, CA 90630.

4. *Steve Taylor*, c/o Sparrow Records, 8025 Deering Avenue, Canoga Park, CA 91304.

5. *A.D.*, c/o BTA Ministries, P.O. Box 158542, Nashville, TN 37215.

6. *Rez Band*, c/o Jesus People USA, 4707 North Malden, Chicago, IL 60640.

7. *U2*, Premier Talent, 3 E. 54th, New York, NY 10022.

8. *Bob Dylan*, P.O. Box 860, Cooper Station, New York, NY 10276.

9. *Donna Summer*, c/o Geffen Records, 9130 Sunset Blvd., Los Angeles CA 90069.

10. *Petra*, Petrafied Productions, P.O. Box 100944, Nashville, TN 37210.

Bibliography

Contemporary Christian music is such a well-kept secret that most American Christians haven't even heard of it.

—*Ted Ojarovsky,* Contemporary Christian Music *magazine*

Some Christians follow the contemporary Christian music scene as locusts follow a drought—devouring every album, every video, every record review. They can rattle off every song title on every album Larry Norman ever made and they know the names and whereabouts of every former Imperials member.

However, *Contemporary Christian Music's* Ted Ojarovsky tells us, "Today's Christian music is a well-kept secret. This makes some people quite unhappy. On the other hand, it makes some people very happy. But no matter what your opinion, the fact is that contemporary Christian music is such a well-kept secret that most American Christians haven't even heard of it."

Ojarovsky says less than one percent of all Christians in this country qualify as Christian music enthusiasts. At most, five percent of all Christians qualify as being moderately aware of Christian music. That means more than ninety percent of today's Christians are unaware such music exists as an alternative to mainstream music.

If you are one of those only moderately aware of the scope of Christian rock—or if you are completely new to the pop gospel scene—you'll appreciate the resources listed on the next few pages.

Periodicals

Truth About Rock Report Bimonthly updates and in-depth reports on secular music's lyrics, lifestyles, goals and graphics, as well as latest Christian contemporary music news and reviews. Write: Truth About Rock, P.O. Box 9222, St. Paul, MN 55109.

Contemporary Christian Music (formerly *Contemporary Christian*) Monthly magazine covering issues vital to contemporary Christians. Includes interviews with artists, and reviews of music from a Christian perspective. Write: Contemporary Christian Music, CCM Publications, Inc., P.O. Box 15427, Santa Ana, CA 92705–0427.

New Christian Media Articles on media and communication as well as extensive interviews with Christian artists from North America and Europe, and relevant music reviews. Write: New Christian Media, Subscriptions Department, 12 Cranston Road, Forest Hill, London SE23 7HT, England. (Be sure to use proper postage.)

Cornerstone No-nonsense, hard-hitting magazine for young adults that will "inform, encourage and challenge." Covers variety of issues as well as interviews and reviews of Christian rock groups. Write: Cornerstone Magazine, 4707 North Malden, Chicago, IL 60640.

Campus Life Action-packed, practical, interesting reading for high school and college-age people, including both secular and Christian rock. Write: Campus Life, Subscription Services, P.O. Box 1947, Marion, OH 43306.

Vortexx "The basic goal of *Vortexx* is to understand how Jesus Christ is perceived by twentieth century man." Bimonthly look at Christian new wave, heavy metal and rock records, videos and concerts. Write: Vortexx, 12129 Genesee St., Alden, NY, 14004.

Media Update Bimonthly publication of Menconi Ministries, specializing in parent/child relationships, media effects on culture, and rock music. Each issue features guest column by Christian rock artist. Write: Menconi Ministries, P.O. Box 306, Cardiff, CA 92007–0831. (619) 436–8676.

Christian Activities Calendar Bimonthly issues include updated regional information on hundreds of concerts; feature stories; record, book and video previews; author and artist interviews. Write: Christian Activities Calendar, P.O. Box 730, Dept. S–301, Ojai, CA 93023.

Teen Vision "Helping teens evaluate and utilize the media and music," *Teen Vision* is newer bimonthly tabloid edited and produced by former Philadelphia Christian radio deejay, Robert "Bobby Dee" DeMoss. Presents both Christian and secular music news, reviews and interviews, column detailing roots of rock. Write: Teen Vision, Subscription Department, P.O. Box 4505, Pittsburgh, PA 15205.

Strait Bible-based bimonthly newspaper from Great Britain, covering film, theater, music (not just rock), politics, and fashion. With interviews of both Christians and non-Christians, thought-provoking discussion and humor, publication is "committed to the development of the Christian mind." Write: The Powerfulnailya Shop, P.O. Box 181, Palmyra, NJ 08065.

The Revealer Inexpensive ("Free to the Max but donations accepted") but fitfully published fanzine offering in-depth interviews with top Christian artists, news briefs, Christian music charts, off-beat humor. Write: The Revealer, 4304 Pollack, Evansville, IN 47715.

Buzz Magazine "Britain's leading Christian monthly magazine," presents Christian artist interviews, regular column by Steve Taylor, media news, CCM charts, music reviews. Write: Buzz, 37 Elm Road, New Malden, KT3 3HB, England. (Be sure to use proper postage.)

Further Reading

Below are books with interesting, sometimes controversial material on both secular and Christian rock music, the media, and other subjects pertaining to young people.

Why Knock Rock? by Dan and Steve Peters with Cher Merrill. A comprehensive, definitive analysis of rock music providing help for young people and parents in making reasoned, biblical decisions about rock music. Published by Bethany House and available from your local bookstore, or write Truth About Rock.

Rock's Hidden Persuader: The Truth About Backmasking by Dan and Steve Peters with Cher Merrill. A reasoned look at the controversial subject of subliminals, with documentation of subliminal messages in rock music as well as advertising. Published by Bethany House and available at your local bookstore, or write Truth About Rock.

Contemporary Christian Music (formerly *Why Should the Devil Have All the Good Music?*) by Paul Baker. This book excels as a history of contemporary Christian music by a former deejay and author of over 400 articles on music. Published by Crossway Books and available at your local Christian bookstore.

The Christian, The Arts, And Truth by Frank E. Gaebelein. With strong, underlying commitment to the authority of Scripture, Gaebelein—an editor, preacher, Bible scholar and connoisseur of the arts—discusses the importance of all the arts and gives guidelines for their enjoyment. Published by Multnomah Press and available from your local bookstore.

The Peters Brothers Hit Rock's Bottom by Dan and Steve Peters. A vivid expose of the real world behind the false image of secular rock music. Write Truth About Rock.

What the Devil's Wrong With Rock Music? (Revised and edited version of *Documentation I*) by Dan and Steve Peters. Quotes, interviews, song lyrics and facts about secular rock stars presented in no-nonsense form. Write Truth About Rock.

Truth About Rock (Expanded, revised and up-dated version of *Documentation II*) by Dan and Steve Peters with Cher Merrill. Crammed with up-to-date information on secular rock stars' lives, intentions, lyrics and LP covers. Write Truth About Rock.

Audio Tapes

What About Christian Rock? By Dan and Steve Peters and Cher Merrill. Hear actual taped interviews with Christian rock's top artists and examples of their music. Dan and Steve draw biblical conclusions that will help teens make informed decisions about Christian rock. Write Truth About Rock.

Why Knock Rock? by Dan and Steve Peters. The original seminar that made national headlines. Revealing 90-minute audio tape details facts and figures on secular rock music's threat to young people. Produced by Bethany House and available at your local bookstore, or write Truth About Rock.

Stryper: Whose Side Are They On? by Dan and Steve Peters. Fascinating, fast-paced audio tape filled with interviews of Christian rock music's most controversial foursome. Write Truth About Rock.

AC/DC: Wanted For Murder by Dan and Steve Peters. Hear shocking testimonies of suicidal teens and the rock songs that urged them to "pull the trigger." Write Truth About Rock.

Rock's Hidden Persuader by Dan and Steve Peters. An audio tape packed with evidence of satanic messages deliberately hidden in rock songs. Actual scientific studies of the effects of subliminals on unsuspecting listeners. Produced by Bethany House and available at your local bookstore, or write Truth About Rock.

Video Tapes and Films

Truth About Rock by Dan and Steve Peters. Made-for-television video of the Truth About Rock Seminar. Great for parents, teens, youth and Sunday school groups. Fast moving, one-hour VHS tape. Write Truth About Rock.

Youth Suicide Fantasy: Does the Music Make Them Do It? Produced by Dan and Steve Peters, written by Cher Merrill and Jan Horton. Two-part series provides chilling facts on youth suicide, provides actual case histories of suicide attempts influenced by rock music. Teaches teens how to survive. Available for sale as VHS tape, or for rent in two-part 16 film. Write Truth About Rock.

Echoes Produced by Word Records, this series includes a 30-minute music and video film, discussion guides on Christian contemporary music, newspapers, cassettes, regular mailings, and a music video lending library, all available to youth pastors and leaders for their youth groups. For more information, write Word Regional Promotion, P.O. Box 1790, Waco, TX, 76796.

Petra Video Petrafied Productions has a video available for youth groups that details the methods and ministry of one of contemporary Christian music's most popular groups. Also available is a Petra newsletter. Write Carol Anderson, Petrafied Productions, P.O. Box 111386, Nashville, TN 37222-1386.

Festivals

More than just giant jam sessions, Christian music festivals can provide solid teaching and time for family fun. The speakers often present a challenge to believers at all levels of maturity and the Christian artists offer wholesome, inspiring entertainment for Christians as well as non-Christians. Below are just a few of the many held in the U.S. and abroad:

SonShine Festival, Willmar, Minnesota. Usually held one weekend in mid-July, this successful festival offers popular Christian speakers, a varied line-up of Christian rock and pop bands, on-site camping. Write: SonShine Productions, 6926 Emerson Avenue, No., Brooklyn Center, MN 55430. (612) 560–6907.

Jesus Joyfest, Agape Campground, Shirleysburg, Pennsylvania. The original "Jesus festival," a "soundly balanced 3-day program of music, ministry, worship." Usually end of July, features more than two dozen speakers and bands, on-site camping. Write: Jesus Ministries, R.D. #1, Box 58B, Shirleysburg, PA 17260. (814) 447–5659.

Greenbelt Festival, Northhamptonshire, England. Since 1974, a four-day affair at Castle Ashby Park, providing a "bridge between the world and the church." Offers music, drama, dance, teaching, top U.S. and European Christian rock groups. Fosters excellence in the arts and opportunity for non-Christians to hear and respond to the Christian call. Write: Greenbelt Festivals, 81 Harley House, Marylebone Road, London NW1, England. (Be sure to use proper postage.)

Fishnet Festival, Front Royal, Virginia. Early July, three-day interfaith camping event, has met near Washington, D.C., for over a decade. Program includes "preaching, teaching, praising, fellowshiping, dynamic music." Write: Fishnet, P.O. Box 1919, Front Royal, VA 22630. (703) 636–2961.

Creation Festival, Mt. Union, Pennsylvania. Late-June event billed "the nation's largest Christian festival." Agape Camp Farm, c/o P.O. Box 86, Medford, NJ 08055. (609) 654–8440.

Cornerstone Festival, Grayslake, Illinois. A relative newcomer first held in 1984, is committed to challenging festival-goers to "translate faith into action." Assembles respected international Christian leaders, hottest U.S. and European bands for four days of rap and rock in early July. Camping available. Write: Cornerstone Festival, c/o Jesus People USA, 4707 North Malden, Chicago, IL 60640. (312) 561–2450.

European Christian Artists Music Seminar, De Bron, Holland. Features more than 50 international artists in disciplines from classical to heavy metal, and scores of lecturers "teaching on everything from a biblical theology of music to instrumental techniques." Early week in August. Write: Christian Artists Seminar, c/o Word Records, Northbridge Road, Berkhamstead, HP4 1 EH, England. (Be sure to use proper postage.)

Agape Festival, Greenville, Illinois. Since 1977, "a celebration of love" featuring Christian rock bands, seminars for youth leaders, speakers, video tent with latest CCM videos. Write: Agape Tickets, 315 E. College, Greenville, IL 62246. (618) 664–1840/Ext. 352.

Kingdom Festival, Orlando, Florida. Usually mid-July event highlighted by top CCM performers and popular speakers. Write: Regal Ventures, P.O. Box 867, Kings Mountain, NC 28086. (704) 739–3838.

Christian Music Festival, Atlanta, Georgia. Top names in Christian music appear at amusement center, dates vary. Write: Christian Music Festival, Six Flags Over Georgia, P.O. Box 43187, Atlanta, GA 30378. (404) 948–9290.

Jesus Northwest, Salem, Oregon. Mid-July festival at Oregon State Fairgrounds, featuring Christian pop artists and speakers appealing to teens. Write: Jesus Northwest, P.O. Box 7718, Salem, OR 97303. (503) 393–1616.

Gospel Music Association Seminar/Dove Awards, Nashville, Tennessee. Early April five-day event providing inspiration, education to music ministries, star-studded nightly concerts and annual Dove Awards presentations. Write: The Gospel Music Association, P.O. Box 23201, Nashville, TN 37202. (615) 242–0303.

Christian Artists' Music Seminar in the Rockies, Estes Park, Colorado. Late July event offers 250 workshops, classes and seminars for Christian performers, songwriting competitions, battle of bands and six daily and nightly concerts. Write: Rockies Artist Seminar, Christian Artists Corporation, Box 1984, Thousand Oaks, CA 91360. (805) 499–4306.

Fellowship of Contemporary Christian Ministries (FCCM) Conference. Annual international conference at various sites, offers new talent showcases and nightly concerts. Write: National FCCM Conference Coordinator, P.O. Box 928, Adrian, MI 49221. (517) 263–6801.

Did you know there is a place in your area where you can discover what's happening in Christian music in your community? It's your local Christian bookstore! It's a great place to get the latest Christian books, records, tapes and videos. But usually bookstores also have a bulletin board or poster wall—the most convenient place to find out what's going on in your area in the way of concerts, speakers and activities. Check it out!

Index

How to Contact the Peters Brothers

Seven countries, 40 states, 1,000 seminars, 1,000,000 attenders—the Peters Brothers will go anywhere to expose youth to the TRUTH ABOUT ROCK.

To schedule a rock music seminar in your area, have your group coordinator, pastor, youth pastor, or other interested seminar host call or write for details:

The Peters Brothers
Truth About Rock
Box 9222
North Saint Paul, MN 55109
(612) 770-8114